First *Chico*
Buarque

33 1/3 Global

33 1/3 Global, a series related to but independent from **33 1/3**, takes the format of the original series of short, music-based books and brings the focus to music throughout the world. With initial volumes focusing on Japanese and Brazilian music, the series will also include volumes on the popular music of Australia/Oceania, Europe, Africa, the Middle East, and more.

33 1/3 Japan

Series Editor: Noriko Manabe

Spanning a range of artists and genres—from the 1970s rock of Happy End to technopop band Yellow Magic Orchestra, the Shibuya-kei of Cornelius, classic anime series *Cowboy Bebop*, J-Pop/EDM hybrid Perfume, and vocaloid star Hatsune Miku—33 1/3 Japan is a series devoted to in-depth examination of Japanese popular music of the twentieth and twenty-first centuries.

Published Titles:

Supercell's *Supercell* by Keisuke Yamada

Yoko Kanno's *Cowboy Bebop Soundtrack* by Rose Bridges

Perfume's *Game* by Patrick St. Michel

Cornelius's *Fantasma* by Martin Roberts

Joe Hisaishi's *My Neighbor Totoro: Soundtrack* by Kunio Hara

Shonen Knife's *Happy Hour* by Brooke McCorkle

Nenes' *Koza Dabasa* by Henry Johnson

Forthcoming Titles:

Yuming's *The 14th Moon* by Lasse Lehtonen

Yellow Magic Orchestra's *Yellow Magic Orchestra* by Toshiyuki Ohwada

Kohaku utagassen: The Red and White Song Contest by Shelley Brunt

33 1/3 Brazil

Series Editor: Jason Stanyek

Covering the genres of samba, tropicália, rock, hip hop, forró, bossa nova, heavy metal and funk, among others, 33 1/3 Brazil is a series devoted to in-depth examination of the most important Brazilian albums of the twentieth and twenty-first centuries.

33 1/3 Europe

Series Editor: Fabian Holt
Spanning a range of artists and genres, 33 1/3 Europe offers engaging accounts of popular and culturally significant albums of Continental Europe and the North Atlantic from the twentieth and twenty-first centuries.

Forthcoming Titles:

Los Rodriguez's *Sin Documentos* by Fernán del Val and Héctor Fouce

Massada's *Astaganaga* by Lutgard Mutsaers

Nuovo Canzoniere Italiano's *Bella Ciao* by Jacopo Tomatis

Amália Rodrigues's *Amália at the Olympia* by Lilla Ellen Gray

Ardit Gjebrea's *Projekt Jon* by Nicholas Tochka

Vopli Vidopliassova's *Tantsi* by Maria Sonevytsky

Édith Piaf's *Recital 1961* by David Looseley

Iannis Xenakis' *Persepolis* by Aram Yardumian

33 1/3 Oceania

Series Editors: Jon Stratton and Jon Dale

Spanning a range of artists and genres, from New Zealand noise music to Australian hip hop, 33 1/3 Oceania offers engaging accounts of popular and culturally significant albums from the 20th and 21st centuries.

Published Titles:

John Farnham's *Whispering Jack* by Graeme Turner

Forthcoming Titles:

Regurgitator's *Unit* by Lachlan Goold and Lauren Istvandity

Ed Kuepper's *Honey Steel's Gold* by John Encarnacao

The Church's *Starfish* by Chris Gibson

Kylie Minogue's *Kylie* by Adrian Renzo and Liz Giuffre

Space Waltz's *Space Waltz* by Ian Chapman

The Dead C's *Clyma est mort* by Darren Jorgensen

Chain's *Toward the Blues* by Peter Beilharz

Bic Runga's *The Drive* by Henry Johnson

The Front Lawn's *Songs from the Front Lawn* by Matthew Bannister

First *Chico Buarque*

Charles A. Perrone

Series Editor: Jason Stanyek

BLOOMSBURY ACADEMIC

NEW YORK • LONDON • OXFORD • NEW DELHI • SYDNEY

BLOOMSBURY ACADEMIC
Bloomsbury Publishing Inc
1385 Broadway, New York, NY 10018, USA
50 Bedford Square, London, WC1B 3DP, UK
29 Earlsfort Terrace, Dublin 2, Ireland

BLOOMSBURY, BLOOMSBURY ACADEMIC and the Diana logo are
trademarks of Bloomsbury Publishing Plc

First published in the United States of America 2022

Copyright © Charles A. Perrone, 2022

For legal purposes the Acknowledgments on pp. xi–xii constitute
an extension of this copyright page.

All rights reserved. No part of this publication may be reproduced or
transmitted in any form or by any means, electronic or mechanical,
including photocopying, recording, or any information storage or retrieval
system, without prior permission in writing from the publishers.

Bloomsbury Publishing Inc does not have any control over, or
responsibility for, any third-party websites referred to or in this book. All
internet addresses given in this book were correct at the time of going
to press. The author and publisher regret any inconvenience caused if
addresses have changed or sites have ceased to exist, but can accept no
responsibility for any such changes.

Whilst every effort has been made to locate copyright holders the
publishers would be grateful to hear from any person(s) not here
acknowledged.

Library of Congress Cataloging-in-Publication Data
Names: Perrone, Charles A., author.
Title: First Chico Buarque / Charles A. Perrone.
Other titles: Chico Buarque
Description: New York : Bloomsbury Academic, 2022. | Series: 33 1/3
Brazil | Includes bibliographical references and index. |
Summary: "A critical account of the eponymous 1978 album by
Chico Buarque, who is widely considered to be one of the greatest
Brazilian popular music artists"– Provided by publisher.
Identifiers: LCCN 2021050102 (print) | LCCN 2021050103 (ebook) |
ISBN 9781501379796 (hardback) | ISBN 9781501379789 (paperback) |
ISBN 9781501379802 (epub) | ISBN 9781501379819 (pdf) |
ISBN 9781501379826 (ebook other)
Subjects: LCSH: Buarque, Chico, 1944-. Chico Buarque (1978) |
Buarque, Chico, 1944—Criticism and interpretation. | Popular music–
Brazil–1971-1980–History and criticism.
Classification: LCC ML410.B923 P47 2022 (print) | LCC ML410.B923
(ebook) | DDC 782.42164092–dc23
LC record available at https://lccn.loc.gov/2021050102
LC ebook record available at https://lccn.loc.gov/2021050103

ISBN: HB: 978-1-5013-7979-6
        PB: 978-1-5013-7978-9
        ePDF: 978-1-5013-7981-9
        eBook: 978-1-5013-7980-2

Series: 33 1/3 Brazil

Typeset by Integra Software Services Pvt. Ltd.
Printed and bound in Great Britain

To find out more about our authors and books visit www.bloomsbury.com
and sign up for our newsletters.

Contents

Preface

The Origins

There are four generally recognized giants among the singer-songwriters of Brazilian popular music who emerged in the late 1960s: Caetano Veloso, Gilberto Gil, Milton Nascimento, and Chico Buarque. In the years following the founding proposal for the *Brazil 33 1/3* catalogue (2014) and its baptism (2017), titles have been published concerning long-play records by the first three of those "big four." A large gap remained to complete the quadrilateral pantheon in this editorial context, and I decided to try to fill it with a contribution on an album by the gentleman whom many consider to be the most important cultural figure of all: Francisco Buarque de Hollanda (b. 1944), stage name and nom-de-plume, Chico Buarque. The first challenge was to decide which musical work to explore, which of his twenty-two studio albums of original material to focus on. His remarkable debut title (1966)? Some retrospective from his late career? (The latest CD is 2011). A loaded self-titled LP, the second to be named *Chico Buarque* (1984), on the eve of Brazil's return to electoral democracy? There were several extremely worthy candidates, but I settled on the first eponymous *Chico Buarque* (1978) for a series of reasons I hope will become clear in the course of this modest monograph. I have used the overall title *First* Chico Buarque to distinguish the chosen 33 1/3 from the later red-cover disc (and another on a different label) of the same name.[1]

The album I have selected may not be the singer-songwriter's "best"—critics and fan polls usually reserve that accolade for the monumental *Construção* (Construction, 1971)—nor does it contain the poet-composer's greatest song—that would be the tripartite "O que será?" (What can it be?) on the 1976 disc *Meus caros amigos* (My dear friends)—but no other LP/CD brings together so many different threads and leads in one place. The first *Chico Buarque* merits consideration and analysis in interrelated contexts, including the artist's own career, the evolution of currents he represents in Brazilian popular music, musical internationalism, and, especially, historical conjuncture. As a collection drawing on diverse sources and resources, the first *Chico Buarque* is not a unified "concept album"—such as *Tropicália ou Panis et Circensis* (1968) by Gil and Veloso et al. or Gil's own Afro-set *Refavela* (1977)—but it is replete with conceptual chords and harmonic conceits, some upfront some not so much, and the totality of the sounds and ideas in play is quite rich and gives a well-rounded idea of the artistic project of Chico Buarque, performing songwriter, playwright, fiction writer, and revered Brazilian icon. The chosen late seventies' album, in short, is outstanding and

---

[1] *Chico Buarque*, Philips Polygram 1978; *Chico Buarque* Polygram-Barclay 1984; *Chico Buarque* BMG Ariola—RCA Victor 1989; see *Discografia* at the official site www.chicobuarque.com.br, the non-chronological all-inclusive Discography at www.discogs.com/artist/312060-Chico-Buarque, and the useful personal site www.slipcue.com/music/brazil/buarque.html, with additional links.

remarkable: there are engaging stories for every track, some more easily explained, others with extensive case files, both in the trade press and in academic indexes. With veritable hymns among songs that look back and others that look forward, this album has exciting convergences and reverberates in multiple directions. It can be considered a truly pivotal item in the domains of Chico Buarque and of the modern popular music of his homeland. As a nod to the count of eleven tracks on the album, this book of appreciation will be divided into eleven editorial segments.

Acknowledgments

First of all *muito obrigado*/much obliged to Jason Stanyek, general editor of the *Brazil 33 1/3* series, for having continued to encourage me, over a span of several years, to submit a proposal. His advice and recommendations at each stage have been invaluable. At the press, thanks are due to Leah Babb-Rosenfeld, Rachel Moore, and everyone involved in the production process, for their patience and assistance. Many people—in North America, Brazil, and elsewhere—have contributed to this project in different ways, providing information, materials, suggestions, clarifications, contacts, inspiration and/or just plain good spirit. I recognize, in alphabetical order: Estrella Acosta, Samuel Araújo, Piers Armstrong, Luca Bacchini, Heather Bergseth, Márcio Borges, Dário Borim, Paulo Henriques Britto, Victoria Broadus, Larry Crook, Christopher J. Dunn, Rinaldo Fernandes, Carlos Galilea Nin, Fred Goes, Jonathon Grasse, James N. Green, Luiz Roberto Guedes, Marc Hertzman, Shuhei Hosokawa, Randal Johnson, Scott Kettner, Jeffrey Lesser, Daniel Touro Linger, Salgado Maranhão, Bryan Mc Cann, Chris Mc Gowan, Zuza Homem de Mello (RIP), Luciana Monteiro, Pedro Meira Monteiro, Brian Moran, Marcos Napolitano, Ricardo Pessanha, Claudio Valladares Pádua, José Augusto Pádua, Adalberto Paranhos, Edimilson de Almeida Pereira, Joachim Polack, Rosane Carneiro Ramos, Carlos Rennó, Evelyn Rosenthal, David Rumpler, Carlos Sandroni, Antonio Carlos Secchin, Gerald Seligman, Daniel Shapiro, Ricardo Silvestrin, David Spiller, Sean Stroud, Ned

Sublette, Daniella Thompson, David Treece, Sandy Tsukiyama, Martha Tupinambá de Ulhôa, André Vallias, and José Miguel Wisnik. My apologies if I have overlooked a deserving soul.

A special memory: Zídia Oliveira Webb, *professora de português*, first introduced me, close to fifty years ago, to the songs of Chico Buarque, not just for listening pleasure, but for their value in the classroom and cultural criticism.

Marola Edições Musicais (Chico Buarque himself and manager Júlia Valladares), Gegê Edições (manager Eveline Alves), and Ojalá Ediciones (Silvio Rodríguez himself and representative Mirtha Almeida) graciously granted permissions to reprint original lyrics and to publish derivative translations. I thank each photographer whose works I have included (or agency authorized to permit use of images); credit is given on the pages where they appear.

As always, for Regina Rheda, *rainha do maracatu do meu coração*.

Thanks to one and all!

1 Intro: Pagings and Stagings

In the pages that follow, the aim is to situate the eponymous, self-titled album *Chico Buarque* (1978), the first *Chico Buarque*, in its times and places, which are plural for personal and public reasons. This release was the artist's ninth studio recording of original material, more than ten years after a rather auspicious debut.[1] For many, he was, and still is, the prime figure in the trend dubbed *MPB* (*música popular brasileira*, Brazilian popular music), an umbrella acronym for a generation of post-bossa nova composers and performers who created their sounds with traditional inspirations and individual imagination alike.[2] While Chico is noted as an absolute genius in the making of song texts, both amatory and socially relevant, he has also penned hundreds of engaging melodies, some uniquely

[1] From this point forward all references to an unmodified *Chico Buarque* are to the 1978 release. By that year Chico had also released LPs of stage songs, a couple of live-in-concert pairings with other stars of his generation, and a collection of tunes for a children's play. Per Brazilian custom, I will refer to the artist by his first name if not both first and last.

[2] For book-length treatments of this topic in English, see Charles A. Perrone, *Masters of Contemporary Brazilian Song: MPB 1965–1985* (Austin: University of Texas Press, 1989); Sean Stroud, *The Defence of Tradition in Brazilian Popular Music: Politics, Culture and the Creation of* Música Popular Brasileira (Burlington VT: Ashgate, 2008). Chapter 1 of the former monograph is "Chico Buarque: A Unanimous Construction."

magnetic. His musical partnerships (co-writing ventures and duets) are also worthy of note.

The cloud hanging over the first twenty-one years of his life in music, and as an adult citizen, was the right-wing military dictatorship in Brazil (1964–1985). *Chico Buarque* was released on the eve of the official beginning of *abertura*—the authoritarian regime's eagerly anticipated political opening after years of stern control—and the music both reflects that hope of redemocratization and comprises, in part, a sonic retrospective on the dark days of severe repression. In the midst of unfolding events, this set of tunes actually performs *abertura*, as censorship was being relaxed and previously banned songs could return to circulation or be released for the first time. Two are today considered historical hymns of protest and resistance. Another pair treats of life in communist Cuba and revolutionary Portugal. Other compositions most effectively exemplify the depth and complexity of the composer's affective text and melodic handiwork. The 1978 collection also previews Chico's next album, the soundtrack to a celebrated social-satire musical, which also became a film. In addition to those pieces that sing of dissent in the 1970s, there are three tunes from that incisive *Ópera do malandro*, which concerns governance and urban change in the 1940s. The *malandro* (rogue, for now) is a prominent figure in popular culture and will be explained more fully below and in the several chapters about songs with such characters.

With the sum of such content, this set of sambas and lyrical compositions is imbued with historical substance and resonance. Keen to the broader range of the artist's individual genius, Brazil's most profound musical critic writes that so many of Chico's songs "comprise—and this is what defines them—beyond an 'agenda' of our contemporary history, an affective and personal agenda that surprises and inscribes, in each collective instance, the mark of an irreductible vertical experience, even if always accompanied by the sensation of being shared."[3] The songs both point to history and are themselves real and symbolic events. In addition to the epoch-marking political anthems, the 1978 tracks amply illustrate an inter-arts imperative: compositions are tied to drama, to film (in the samba overture), to regional culture and literary modernism, and to socialist expression abroad. The motives to consider this particular content-laden album, again, are manifold.

Chico Buarque was born in Rio de Janeiro on June 19, 1944. The family soon moved to the metropolis of São Paulo, where his father, the illustrious historian Sérgio Buarque de Holanda (1902–82), got a prestigious job. He later took a visiting professorship in Italy, where the family resided for several years. At home, son Chico always mingled with intellectuals and artists, most notably the diplomat, Modernist poet and foundational figure of bossa nova, Vinícius de Moraes (1913–80). Like so many others in the late 1950s, the young Chico wanted to emulate the doyen of nascent bossa nova,

---

[3] José Miguel Wisnik, "O arista e o tempo." In José Miguel Wisnik *Sem receita: ensaios e canções* (São Paulo: Publifolha, 2004), p. 243. This piece was co-written with son Guilherme to serve as introduction to volume 3 of a didactic volume, see note 13. The segment was translated by local staff but I use my own translation here, as I do throughout unless otherwise noted.

singer-guitarist João Gilberto. After high school, he began to study architecture at the college level in São Paulo, but his true calling was music, and so it would be. His career paralleled historical events. It was in 1964 that the military deposed the democratically elected president João Goulart and installed a dictatorial regime that would exert power for twenty-one years. From the outset, the unassuming talent composed both sentimental and social/political songs, but it was the latter kind that got him in trouble with authorities and led to a titanic battle of wills for several years. In 1966, Chico's alluring march "A banda" (The band) shared first place at one of the landmark festivals that marked the history of song in the late 1960s.[4] The gracious victor earned himself a reputation as a relatively reserved and well-behaved gentleman, not to mention a contract with a major label. That standard image of a respectful citizen would not last long. His 1967–8 play *Roda viva* (Spinning wheel/Rat race) presented a grim view of the music business, and one of the performances was attacked by right-wing thugs. However, Chico's appeal was inexorably broad and profound. His songs incorporated both bossa nova and the finest legacy of samba. He was compared to, even called the legitimate heir of, the genius songsmith Noel Rosa (1910–37), "The Philosopher of Samba" who did

---

[4] The most complete source for this topic is Zuza Homem de Mello, *A era dos festivais: uma parábola* (São Paulo: editora 34 Letras, 2003). There is no dedicated monograph in English, but there are good brief accounts in such sources as Christopher Dunn, *Brutality Garden: Tropicália and the Emergence of a Brazilian Counter Culture* (Chapel Hill: University of North Carolina Press, 2001), especially p. 61 ff.

so much to help make the genre a sophisticated mode of national expression.[5]

When a Chico Buarque box set was released in 1994 to commemorate the recording artist's half century in the business, selections from some thirty albums were organized into five groups (a CD each): (1) *o malandro* [the rogue]; (2) *o trovador* [the troubador]; (3) *o amante* [the lover]; (4) *o cronista* [the chronicler]; (5) *o político* [the political man]. With the exception of #2, for some unfathomable reason, two tunes from the 1978 LP were part of each thematic disc. Truth be told, lines of separation between these categories are not always so clear. Whether for their sonorous character or textual content, musical compositions can be associated simultaneously with a love affair and social conditions, with narrative or lyrical modes, with anti-normative behavior and other territories, and so on. Such ambiguities are testament to the depth of Chico's production. In the course of the chapters that follow each of these categories will figure in. Since *malandro* is the first category brought to bear, we best get to it forthwith.

An oft-analyzed social type in Brazil, the *malandro* is a recurring presence in the emergence and evolution of

---

[5] English language sources include Bryan McCann, "Noel Rosa's Nationalist Logic." *Luso-Brazilian Review*, vol. 38, no. 1 (2001), pp. 1–16; his wider-ranging monograph *Hello, Hello, Brazil: Popular Music in the Making of Modern Brazil* (Durham: Duke University Press, 2004); Lisa Shaw, "Samba and Brasilidade: Notions of National Identity in the Lyrics of Noel Rosa." *Lusotopie*, vol. 2 (2002), pp. 81–96; and a convenient academic translation: Leandro Moreira da Luz, Bruno Flávio Lontra Fagundes, Mônica Luiza Sócio Fernandes, "The Samba Controversy between Noel Rosa and Wilson Batista: Intertextuality and the Meanders of Composition." *Bakhtiniana: Revista de Estudos do Discurso*, vol. 10, no. 2 (2015), pp. 36–53. https://doi.org/10.1590/2176-457320986.

the foundational Brazilian genre that is samba. He is also a frequent character in the songs of Chico Buarque. If one looks in various Portuguese-English dictionaries or glossaries the definitions will include loafer, bum, good-for-nothing, vagabond, rascal, sharper, scamp, scoundrel. Academics also use "urban hustler." In the nineteenth century, the base meaning of the term was already he who did not work, was not gainfully employed, and did not live according to social norms or the law. By the 1920s—after abolition, the formation of the Brazilian republic, mass migration to the cities, urbanization, social stratification, widespread unemployment, the surge of urban subcultures—the image of the *malandro* took on other associations, notably with such behavioral stances as ostentation (sartorial, attitudinal), resistance to domestic life, carefree relaxation, survival by one's wits (gambling, hustling), and involvement with samba. The classic malandro represented "astuteness and ingenuity, a mix of marginality and cool moves, more a style of life than a survival strategy."[6] The often knife-wielding malandro prized his straw hat and living off of others. Pedro Meira Monteiro notes with more specificity:

> Sometimes translated as "rogue," the *malandro* has become a stereotypical figure of the Brazilian—more specifically *carioca*, or Rio de Janeiro-born—individual who bounces and dribbles so as to swerve around the law, surviving in a space that the state usually fails to reach completely. The character was

---

[6] Fernando de Barros e Silva, *Chico Buarque* (São Paulo: Publifolha, 2004), p. 84.

personified in the 1940s by Walt Disney's Zé, or Joe Carioca, a *malandro* parrot from Rio.[7]

Thus, *malandro* can be associated with anyone who games the system, and with show business as well. In the arts, as on the streets, it might be a type of "trickster" who uses subterfuge to his advantage or to communicate sensitive content. The translator of a classic essay on the *malandro* in Brazilian literature found that all these renderings of the term left "something to be desired" and chose to leave the word in Portuguese and let readers "fill in its meaning contextually."[8] Such an approach will prove to be convenient here too as we unpack the LP *Chico Buarque*, for each of the songs that evokes the *malandro*—literally or figuratively, explicitly or implicitly, in the voice of a character or a narrator, or in the strategy of the composer—does so in a way somewhat different from the rest of the cohort.

---

[7] Pedro Meira Monteiro, *The Other Roots: Wandering Origins in* Roots of Brazil *and the Impasses of Modernity in Ibero-America*. Trans. Flora Thomson-Deveaux (Notre Dame, IN: University of Notre Dame Press, 2017), p. 219. The essayist refers several times to the works of fiction by Chico Buarque in this monograph. Not counting one short story in his first songbook (1966) and an Orwell-esque novella in 1974, his literary endeavors are later in his career: the short novel *Estorvo* (1991; *Turbulence*, 1993), *Budapest* (2003; trans. 2004), and *Leite derramado* (2009; *Spilled Milk*), and one later surprise. See gloss of *malandro* and artistic summary in the able blog post: https://www.musicandliterature. org/features/2014/7/10/chico-buarque-brazils-malandro-and-icon. The above use of *rogue* is attributable to the translation of a widely cited work of Brazilian anthropology, Roberto DaMatta, *Carnivals, Rogues, and Heroes: An Interpretation of the Brazilian Dilemma*. Trans. John Drury (Notre Dame, IN: University of Notre Dame Press, 1992).

[8] Howard S. Becker, trans. and ed., Antonio Candido, *On Literature and Society* (Princeton, NJ: Princeton University Press, 1995), p. 102. Note to the essay "Dialectic of Malandro-ism."

It is essential to state, in any case, that this type, and its link with the playing of samba, is at the heart of Chico Buarque's celebrated stance as a critic of socio-historical conditions. David Treece, perspicacious as always, has situated this posture in history:

> Chico's preferred musical idiom and rhythmic style for his coded songs of revolt and solidarity, as is well known, was samba—precisely the tradition which the regime had sought to appropriate for its ideological purposes of projecting an image of national well-being and consensus, drawing on its associations with the celebration of carnival and the idea of social mobility embodied in the figure of the mulatto *malandro*. [...] Chico's songs aimed to reclaim its ethos of playful, euphoric celebration as the expression of a popular identity in resistance to, rather than in collusion with, the official culture of the state.[9]

What Treece refers to as "coded songs" are ones in which the text uses "codes"—figurative language, indirect discourse, linguistic subterfuge—to convey messages and/ or sentiments, usually combative. Brazilian journalists and academics have been commenting on such strategies since the 1970s. In 1974, Caetano Veloso wrote the samba "Festa imodesta" (Immodest party), a shout-out to clever songwriters (with allusions to Noel Rosa). The song was intended for Chico to include on his LP *Sinal fechado* (Red light), title of an inventive song by Paulinho da Viola (1969)

---
[9] David Treece, *Brazilian Jive: From Samba to Bossa and Rap* (London: Reaktion Books, 2013), p. 184.

depicting disaffection and perchance fear.[10] All the tracks were compositions by others, as the lead singer was experiencing quite a bit of trouble with government watchdogs, making it difficult to record his own (likely to be censored) material. One of the tunes was actually by two fictitious pseudonyms he contrived to get around censors. Invoking one of them by name, psychoanalyst-journalist Maria Rita Kehl believes that move was particularly inspiring: "What would become of our fantasy of the Brazil of boosterism, militarism, and intimidation in the years that followed without the malandro-ism of Julinho da Adelaide?"[11]

Inspired by one of Caetano's verses, sociologist Gilberto Vasconcellos characterized the oblique way of saying things as *linguagem da fresta* (language of gaps/cracks). Underlining the need to "read between the lines," he establishes a co-relation between acrobatic songwriting in the 1970s and the *malandro* figure of the days of Noel Rosa, whom Chico sought to emulate:

> The *malandro* composer is no longer the one with a scarf around his neck, and a knife in his pocket, like in the times of Noel, but rather he who knows how to pronounce, that is, who knows how to outwit the siege of the censors. […] To say or not to say is simply, in this day and age, a false alternative. What

---

[10] Paulinho's was one of six song texts, including one of Chico's, translated into English as part of an ambitious German project on translation: https://www.toledo-programm.de/cities_of_translators/1586/charles-perrone-six-brazilian-songs. In 1986 Caetano and Chico performed the song "Festa imodesta" on their TV Globo program.

[11] Maria Rita Kehl, "Chico Buarque." In Arthur Nestrovski, ed. *Música popular brasileira hoje* (São Paulo: Publifolha, 2002), p. 61. The cited name is, just to be clear, Chico's invented lyricist.

is important is to know how to pronounce [fast/smooth/slick talk], thus the need to keep an eye on the gaps in MPB.[12]

By 1978, Chico Buarque—romantic and rebel alike—was already somewhat of a national institution. In the estimation of Almir Chediak—the country's number one guitar teacher and editor of a renowned series of songbooks of the compositions of the leading names of bossa nova and MPB—Chico was one of the most successful recording artists of his day to judge by airplay, as five or six tracks of many of his albums in the late 1960s and 1970s could be heard on the radio. Chediak was absolutely taken with the "quality of songs that seek popular taste" and regarded Chico as "one of the dearest and most respected songwriters in all social classes, a success that can be attributed not only to his talent and charisma but also to his acts as a citizen."[13] These qualities certainly shine on the LP *Chico Buarque*. As Chediak was publishing his Chico songbooks, a powerful indication of Chico's lofty public status was his election by readers of the weekly news magazine *Isto é* as *o músico do século* (the musician of the century) in 1999. As a lyricist, Chico has left countless memorable lines. In the age of internet, a heavy-traffic website compiled his forty best phrases; eight were from the 1978 album.[14] Such examples of recognition abound and further attest to the status of the 33 1/3 treated in the present monograph.

---

[12] Gilberto Vasconcellos, *Música popular: de olho na fresta* (Rio de Janeiro: Graal, 1977), p. 72.

[13] Almir Chediak, *Songbook Chico Buarque*, vol. 1 (Rio de Janeiro: Lumiar, 1999), p. 6. This is a three-volume set, each with a distinct critical introduction, conveniently bilingual.

[14] www.letras.mus.br./blog/frases-chico-buarque.

The current that Chico personifies, MPB, was born in the wake of the second generation of makers of bossa nova who wanted to get beyond a perceived sense of alienation in the practice of the style and to incorporate content more in tune with "the people." The *B* (i.e. Brazilian) in the acronym MPB was to emphasize national substance, as opposed to the imitation of rock'n'roll and its local version, Jovem Guarda (Young guard), as well as to evince displeasure with the military regime, seen to be allied with USAmerican imperialism. From the point of view of reception and identity, Carlos Sandroni writes that liking MPB meant having a certain idea of the "Brazilian people" and "republican ideals" (i.e. anti-monarchy and pro-democracy). He continues explaining the cross of music and politics:

> This political and aesthetic knot found in music a privileged means of expression throughout the 1970s, marked by censorship and democratic struggles. The figure of Chico Buarque de Hollanda is paradigmatic here. I stress that the link here works not only for his political songs. To enjoy listening to Chico Buarque and to be fond of his aesthetic implied the election of a certain universe of values and references that embedded a number of republican conventions crystallized in MPB, even in the instances where his lyrics were far from politics.[15]

---

[15] Carlos Sandroni, "Farewell to MPB." In Idelber Avelar and Christopher Dunn, eds. *Brazilian Popular Music and Citizenship* (Durham, NC: Duke University Press, 2011), p. 68. Sandroni's foundational book of historical urban ethnomusicology *Feitiço decente: transformações do samba no Rio de Janeiro (1917–1933)* (Rio de Janeiro: Zahar, 2001) has appeared in English translation by Michael Iyanaga as, *Respectable Spell: Transformations of Samba in Rio de Janeiro* (Champaign-Urbana: University of Illinois Press, 2021).

Beginning in the highly politicized 1960s, into the transitional decade of the 1970s when the album featured in this study appeared, and forward into the twenty-first century, all sorts of elements, beyond the political and extra-political draws, have contributed to Chico Buarque's enduring

Figure 1 Front cover of *Isto é,* issue #1535, December 1999; Chico Buarque, The Musician of the Century, courtesy of editora3, São Paulo, Brazil.

popularity with multiple constituencies. He is from a privileged background but is attentive to the lives of the subaltern and working-class people. He is white but identifies with the majority black and brown Brazilian populace. He is decidedly male but able to compose from female points of view. He hails from metropolitan Rio de Janeiro and São Paulo but is hip to rural and regional referents. He came up as an amateur musician but was able to rub elbows with fully literate and trained professionals. He can play the roles of a bohemian or footballer (soccer man) but is versed in literature and, following in his father's footsteps, social science and history. All of these dualities are food for thought when the subject is Chico Buarque, or the words and music of the first *Chico Buarque*.

2 The Product: Data and Strata

Chico Buarque's first *Chico Buarque*—catalogue number Philips 6349 398, produced and distributed by Polygram Brazil—was recorded on sixteen tracks in the Phonogram studio in greater Rio de Janeiro. It was released in November 1978 in time for the end-of-the-year holiday gift season, with advanced sales and orders reaching 200,000, a rather prodigious number for the local market in which 250,000 constituted platinum level for a national act.[1] In the month it was released it was number twelve on the best-seller list for LPs in Brazil by home-grown talent.

The front cover has the eponymous title and sports a small Philips logo in the upper right-hand corner, but it is almost entirely comprised of a simple color photograph of the artist, more on this meaningful depiction below. The back cover is all black, save for a centered reduced version of the photo and a small-print *ficha técnica* (literally, technical index card) at the bottom, with production credits. (More on the evocative back cover below as well). Inside the standard 30.5-cm square

---

[1] There are sources that list 600,000 pre-sales, but that is an apparent confusion with total sales numbers for the 1976 LP *Meus caros amigos*, to which Chico and his label would naturally aspire again in 1978.

thin cardboard cover there is a booklet, actually a single square sheet printed on both sides, listing tracks, times, lyrics, musicians, and arrangers. This data-lyric sheet's light gray background has a faint watermark reproduction of the cover photo, in almost ghostly fashion.

The total time of the eleven tracks of the first *Chico Buarque* is 32:45, five on Side A for 16:30, and six on Side B for 16:15. English translations of the titles will be provided in the individual chapters (segments/"tracks") to follow. The first and last cuts are straight-ahead sambas, tone-setting bookends as it were. Other compositions belong to a variety of genres and are of varied provenance. The opening tune, from a 1976 movie soundtrack, is "Feijoada completa" (Complete bean stew meal) (Chico Buarque) 2:50, subject of Chapter 4. The second cut is "Cálice" (Cup/chalice) (Gilberto Gil-Chico Buarque) 4:00, a stirring but previously unrecorded 1973 song featuring the stellar vocalist Milton Nascimento, extended topic of Chapter 9. The third track is "Trocando em miudos" (Spelling things out) (Francis Hime-Chico Buarque) 2:50, a sad ballad; the co-writer team, capable of last minute cooperation before entering the studio, is considered in Chapter 5. The bolero "O meu amor" (My love) (Chico Buarque) 4:00, comes fourth and features two special-quest female vocalists. Side A concludes with the samba "Homenagem ao malandro" (Homage to the rogue) (Chico Buarque) 2:50, one of the three titles from Chico's stage musical, seen as a set in Chapter 6.

The flip side opens with the waggish "Até o fim" (Until the end) (Chico Buarque) 2:24, a sort of folk *maracatu* to be appreciated in Chapter 7. The somber chamber piece "Pedaço de mim" (Piece of me) (Chico Buarque) 3:16, is the third stage song. The street samba "Pivete" (Lil' hood) (Francis Hime-Chico Buarque) 2:27 is their second collaboration on this album. In Chapter 8, we take a look at the next two tracks: "Pequeña serenata diurna" (Small daytime serenade) (Silvio Rodriguez) 2:21, unique cover of a contemporary Cuban song, and "Tanto mar" (So much sea) (Chico Buarque) 1:54, a re-write of a 1975 song dedicated to major changes in Portugal. The final cut, focus of Chapter 10, is one of Brazil's most storied ever, "Apesar de você (In spite of you) (Chico Buarque) 3:35. Chapter 11 will consider the sum of these items.

Ideally, an album release by a prominent singer-songwriter should contain all new original songs, especially earlier on in one's career. In the 1960–70s, record deals in Brazil, as elsewhere, commonly stipulated—or there was mutual agreement between parties—that the artist should launch at least an LP per year. If fresh material was not available or other circumstances interfered, artists under contract and labels could decide to issue a recording of a live concert or covers, which Chico Buarque in fact did in the mid-1970s. Another option was to assemble titles from other projects. The 1976 release was *Meus caros amigos* (My dear friends), understood to mean those who commissioned or co-wrote compositions or did duets with Chico for the album; four tracks are from films, three from plays. Several connections, but not as many as for the 1978 LP, when he ended up doing something similar and more. He surely did not want to do another live-in-concert or covers album, but he did not have a lot of time at his disposal to write new songs, as he was exceptionally busy, occupied with the preparation and debut of his musical *Ópera do malandro*. When it was time to get a next collection together and commit to recording, he realized he would have to draw on varied sources. So, he would revisit a banned single ('45) from 1970, finally record a co-written protest song from 1973, rewrite a proscribed carol from 1975, employ a samba from a 1976 film, borrow in advance three pieces from his opera (the entire score would be a double album the next year), cover a Cuban counterpart, call on a trusted co-writing partner to re-do something they had done a year before plus rush to complete a new idea, and even compose live (improvise for keeps in the recording studio). The results cobbled together may not seem wholly unified, but the diverse connections of the compositions proved to make for quite a rewarding experience. Historical resonances and allusions are not just in the songs, but in the album art too.

The front cover seems innocuous enough: looking at the beholder is a green-eyed Chico with a soft smile, cut and combed hair, shaven face, and pin-striped dull-white shirt with collar and top buttons undone revealing a little chest hair, the only potentially spicy detail. Those who had been following the artist's releases in the tumultuous decade could not help but notice a contrast with previous album photos, which presented a mustached man with attitude, maybe a taxi-driver cap, hands on hips or up to his ear, mouth agape or with a wry smile. This 1978 view was, in contrast, somewhat of a throwback to Chico's initial couple of years as a rising star, when he was regarded as *um bom moço*, a fine young man, the toast of the town. He was "the only national unanimity" in the words of a leading columnist. As two reliable chroniclers put it, listening to Chico (1965–8) gave some people hope that things would soon return to the good old days (pre-dictatorship) and pleased all: "Old or young, rich or poor, communists or capitalists, everybody loved Chico, the nice green-eyed young singer."[2] Twelve years after he burst upon the national scene with "A banda" Chico again seemed more cheerful. The fresh album cover photo was, to employ an intra-repertory allusion and in the words of a record-label spokesperson, like that of a kid, "a cara de 'A banda,'" i.e. the spitting image of him at the time of his inaugural big hit.[3] Such a pose was inviting and intriguing.

The detail of green eyes, often brought up as part of the singer's attractive look, relates to the background of the 1978 portrait: an out-of-focus fern, definitely verdant. The image made enough of an impression over the years to lend a convenient nickname to the self-titled album: *o disco da samambaia* (the fern disc). Consumers of Chico born in the 1940s or 1950s may have never heard or used that moniker, but Chico himself employed the term years later.[4] The label must have liked the fern-backed countenance look, as a 1983 compilation—*A arte maior de Chico Buarque*—used an

---

[2] Chris McGowan and Ricardo Pessanha, *The Brazilian Sound: Samba, Bossa Nova and the Popular Music of Brazil*. Revised and expanded edition (Philadelphia: Temple University Press, 2009), p. 84.

[3] Chico Buarque (interview) qtd. by Ana Maria Bahiana, "Cara nova disco novo." *O globo* November 12, 1978. In the Chico Buarque archive at www.jobim.org/chico. See Chapter 3 on the photographer.

[4] In an interview (Radio El Dorado September 27, 1989) transcribed at www.chicobuarque.com.br. Having found, to my surprise, quite a few twenty-first-century uses of the moniker in the course of the research for this book, I consulted numerous listeners closer to my age (70) and only one journal editor admitted to being at all familiar with *samambaia* as an alternate name for the 1978 LP.

alternate take from that photo session framed by gold leaf as the cover art.

While it was the photographer who chose, from several available options at the studio, the fern backdrop for the head shot, one does not know who—the artist, the producer, the cover design artist, the photographer, or some combination thereof—might be the party(ies) responsible for the overall 1978 graphic design (front and back covers, photo dimensions, additional elements, printed data, etc.). Yet there can be symbolic import of the defining component independent of credit. *Samambaia* can be a symbol of persistence, perseverance and capacity, as the fern is a rustic plant that can thrive in hostile environments. Promoters of tattoos might argue that people who use this sign want to show that they have experienced as much. That would qualify as pertinent to Chico's relationship with censors for most of the 1970s. Dream journal purveyors might speculate that when *samambaias* appear green, pretty and healthy, it is a fortunate oneiric foreshadowing of future good dealings. If it were the contrary (drooping plants) there would be a warning that family problems might afflict the dreamer. Chico's ferns are not faded enough to warrant as much. Advertisers for plant sales affirm that ferns mark presence, creating a mini-forest to absorb negative energy from the atmosphere or people present. Chico's smile and spruced-up look might attest to that. However much one wants to read into this album cover, no doubt remains that its simple makeup evinces more than a simple reaction.

The back cover in black, in turn, can be read in terms of censorship history. The space on back covers was commonly used for liner notes, lyrics, photos of the recording session, additional art. An all-black field (save the photo reduction and company data) prompts wonder. It is not hard to attribute the choice to previous events, in the press and government agencies. In Chico's world, the chromatic curtain echoes travails in 1973 when he tried to market an LP of the songs of the drama he co-wrote with Mozambican film director Ruy Guerra: *Calabar, o elogio da traição* (Calabar, in praise of treason), a historical play about a Brazilian who sided with the invading Dutch enemy against the Portuguese colonial power. The stage production itself was not banned until the eve of its debut, causing as much financial distress as possible for the producers. The censors also prohibited the press from revealing this action! As for the music, the label submitted the songwriters' endeavors to the censorship board, who cut "objectionable" (political or erotic) lines from several songs and banned others outright, which had to be recorded as instrumentals. Despite such trouble, the album came out. The original cover, as on the book of the dramatic text, featured the name CALABAR in dripping white paint (like a protest graffiti) on an exterior wall, which was too much for the military's ideological watchdogs, who ordered a stop to distribution.[5] Solution? Re-issue the record with an all-white cover, clearly suggestive of whitewashing and wiping the slate clean. Problem? the public was suspicious and sales were too low

[5] Music and drama were subject to extreme censorship in the period late 1968 – mid 1978, literature not so much given the much smaller number of consumers. Song lyrics and dramatic texts faced *censura prévia* (prior censorship), meaning they had to be submitted for approval to a government agency before public release. Censors could demand changes or ban outright.

to permit the status to continue. Next step? Devise a third and definitive cover with the harmless name *Chico canta* (sings). The fuller name *Chico canta Calabar* (CCC) was not acceptable because CCC suggested *Comando de Caça aos Comunistas* [Communist hunt command], a domestic terrorist group who had, among other ignominious acts, invaded a performance of Chico's play *Roda viva* in 1968. One thing the censors overlooked, however, was the center label of the disc, which read, in full, *Chico canta Calabar, o elogio da traição*. The album went on to sell relatively well, became the stuff of legend, and enjoyed a fourth vinyl iteration in 2019.

The almost all-black back cover in 1978 can be seen as a reverse allusion to the episode of the ill-fated all-white cover of the *Calabar* album five years earlier, and as a reminder of the recent *trevas* (darkness), the tenebrous period of the *anos de chumbo* (the leaden years), the worst stretch of the dictatorship. That sad period suffered terrible persecution of the press as well. The military regime was relatively "bland" during the first years, but after four and a half years of resistance, they brought down the hammer in December 1968 with the infamous AI-5 (Fifth Institutional Act), a decree to institute absolute and brutal control. Soon newspapers and magazines had stories cut right and left. A leading daily in São Paulo resorted to printing daily runs with empty (white) space to indicate that the censors had prevented them from publishing something. After they banned that practice too, the paper would publish recipes or passages from classical literature to signal something askew. Others resorted to black columns, blocks, or boxes (perhaps with some wee innocent advertising messages) to indicate intervention. The non-mainstream journal *Opinião* (Opinion)

Figure 2 Chico Buarque LP and sheet music covers at the offices of
Arlequim music publisher, São Paulo, Brazil (1968); photo by Maurice
Gaulmin, courtesy of owner-operator Waldemar Jorge
Menendez Marchetti.

did a lot of this, as at one point half of all their stories on Brazil
were not allowed.[6] For those sensitive to unfolding events
in the 1970s, this kind of all-too-common maneuvering was

_____

[6] http://memorialdademocracia.com.br/card/opiniao-um-jornal-mutilado-
pela-censura.

recalled, metonymically, by the backcover of the first *Chico Buarque*. On the upside, Chico's smile in the photo box had something to do with changes for the better.[7]

---

[7] The LP was released just after the legal overturning of the justifications of the AI-5, which on October 13, 1978, were reversed by a congressional constitutional amendment to take effect on the first day of 1979. On Brazilian press woes, see Joan Dassin, "Press Censorship—How and Why." *Index on Censorship*, vol. 4 (1979), pp. 13–19.

3 PPP: Persons, Personnel, and Paraphernalia

Another aspect of the first *Chico Buarque* that merits attention is the panoply of personnel assembled: the producer, the star artist, his writing partners, the arrangers, the studio musicians, and, above all, the guest appearances, which add glamour to the release with figures who establish links with other musical projects, historical moments, and regional identities. Those who contributed are documented track by track on the record's insert, not in a separate section at the end as is sometimes the case.

The first impression of a traditional 33 1/3 album, of course, is the front cover, the fern-backed photo of a crisp Chico in this case. The man with a sharp eye and a camera was an up-and-coming music-studio photographer named Januário Garcia Filho (b. Belo Horizonte 1943, d. Rio de Janeiro 2021), who in the 1970s added popular music to his areas of activity as a freelancer, mostly for the press. Starting in 1975, he did photo shoots for Antônio Carlos Jobim, Caetano Veloso, Tim Maia, and dozens of other samba and MPB recording artists. He went on to gain national and international recognition in advertising, Brazilian popular music, and the documentation of Afro-Brazilian life.[1]

[1] See album-cover examples and other data at his recently launched (2021) website www.januariogarcia.com.br—which lists shows around the world and work under the rubrics of *carnaval*, the quotidian, and religiosity, especially of Afro descendant populations, his specialty.

The producer of the first *Chico Buarque* was the well-versed Sérgio de Carvalho (1949–2019) who co-mixed the tapes as well. Followers of Anglo-American rock might be interested to know that he had previously produced a project with Leon Russell and Brazilian players (in an RCA studio), as well as two tracks for a solo recording by one Mick Jagger. In 1976, Carvalho created the series *Música Popular Brasileira Contemporânea* for the PolyGram label, an important step for national jazz (what Brazilians usually call "instrumental music"). Before the 1978 LP, he already had quite a track record with Chico: in addition to the musical direction of television specials in Portugal and Brazil, he headed the sound/overall production of Chico's albums in 1973, 1974, and 1976, *Meus caros amigos*, which has significant ties to the next studio album.

On the record insert, the first credit for each song is voice, indicating the lead singer. Chico Buarque is named on ten of the eleven tracks. He has never been known as a particularly impressive vocalist, but he does have a distinctive sound and a certain unique appeal as author of the songs, much like Bob Dylan.[2] Jobim, the absolute genius of bossa nova composition, is not himself primarily noted as a singer, but he did score a duet gig with The Voice, Frank Sinatra. The composer of "Desafinado," "The Girl from Ipanema," and other classics co-wrote several outstanding songs with the younger Brazilian

[2] Accomplished UK writer David Spiller wrote a personal analysis of the top twenty vocalists in the (Anglophone save one) world: *Great Singers of the 20th Century*. Independent (Amazon Kindle). 2020. Dylan is early on the list and Chico Buarque, the lone non-Anglophone, is last. The vetting is based on the acts themselves and "technical elements of their art." He also authored twenty smart translations of song texts: chicobuarquetranslated.com, or Amazon kindle; only one of these is from the 1978 LP.

star Chico, whom he has called "a good singer."[3] Chico also achieves a high level of emotional communication of his song, no small feat.[4] He is listed on music information sites as a guitarist, but he only plays the instrument on one track here ("Até o fim"). To hear him accompany himself on six-string acoustic guitar one should listen to live recordings. While he has always demonstrated a naturally splendid musical imagination for melody and harmony, his formal training came late. When he first took the qualification examination for the Order of Musicians, the professional union, he failed. It is no surprise that Chico should seek collaborators with full musical expertise.

The main man when it comes to working with Chico has been composer-arranger-pianist Francis Hime (b. 1939), who did half of the arrangements on the 1978 LP and played piano on five cuts. As noted earlier, he also co-wrote two of the tracks. All in all, he has fifteen shared compositions with Chico, second only to Edu Lobo, with whom Chico has two entire albums of songs for dramatic projects. Hime was the musical director on four of Chico's albums. "Trocando em miudos," one of their co-written tunes on the first *Chico Buarque,* was used in the title of Hime's memoir: *Trocando em miudos as minhas canções* (Spelling things out in my songs) (Rio de Janeiro: Terceiro Nome, 2018). The very first song they did together "Atrás da porta" (Behind the door, 1972) is considered one of

[3] Chris McGowan, *The Brazilian Music Book: Brazil's Singers, Songwriters and Musicians Tell The Story of Bossa Nova, MPB, and Brazilian Jazz and Pop* (Santa Monica: Culture Planet, 2012), p. 66.
[4] I owe the wording of this impression to David Rumpler, Brazilian music specialist in Somerville, Massachusetts.

Chico's best sentimental songs, and the last, "Vai passar" (It's on its way/It will pass, 1984) is a historic *samba-enredo* a theme-song for a fictitious samba school, and, thanks in no small part to Hime, Chico's most musically sophisticated samba.

Other arrangers on the first *Chico Buarque* included Magro (Antônio José Waghabi Filho, 1943–2012)—he of the venerable vocal quartet MPB4, who sing on the two songs that had been composed earlier in the decade, "Cálice" and "Apesar de você" (the latter with the additional backing of the all-female Quarteto em Cy)—conductor (Lindolfo) Gaya (1911–1986), Chico himself along with the impromptu band on "Até o fim," and none other than Milton Nascimento. This superstar is known as the incomparable male voice of MPB. He doubles vocal parts with Chico on "Cálice," which was co-written by Gilberto Gil. The two Afro-descendant singer-songwriters have a noteworthy musical relationship as well.[5] Milton also plays piano on the 1978 track he orchestrated "Pedaço de mim." On *Meus caros amigos* (1976), the two superstars had sung Chico's amazing song "O que será," often considered (one of) the best Brazilian songs ever and a landmark of musical history. The significance of the inclusion of Milton is suggested by the critical assessment of a dedicated urban ethnomusicologist: "Milton's soaring voice is one of the most distinctive sounds of MPB, whose music would become a symbol of national identity during the transition to democracy in the mid 1980s."[6] Milton also brought along some of the musicians from the musical

[5] Marc Hertzmann, *Gilberto Gil's* Refazenda (New York: Bloomsbury, 2020), p. 103 ff.

[6] Martha Ulhôa Carvalho, "Canção da América—Style and Emotion in Brazilian Popular Song." *Popular Music*, vol. 9, no. 3 (1990), p. 49.

cohort of Minas Gerais state, the Clube da Esquina: Beto Guedes (bass, mandolin), Novelli (bass, piano and percussion), and Nelson Ángelo (guitar), and all three on percussion.[7]

The next two guest vocalists on the album are Marieta Severo and Elba Ramalho, who sing the two female roles from the stage song "O meu amor." The former was Chico's wife (1966–99) and had worked with him on the controversial play *Roda viva*. In addition to the theatre, she worked in film and television. Elba Ramalho was a soon-to-be-star singer from the Northeast with an energetic style. She would go on to record dozens of albums of her own. The duet would be reprised on the double album of the malandro opera. Zizi Possi was also just beginning in the business when she got the chance to add her vocals to "Pedaço de mim," joining Chico in a duet. The reception was good enough that the name of the song was used as the title of her second LP a year later. The three women on *Chico Buarque* are all singing as feminine characters created by the songwriter; thus, they are part of a career-long aspect of his output that has fascinated listeners and analysts: incisive words of women composed by a musical man.[8]

The producer was busy for these sessions. He hired over fifty studio musicians for the 1978 dates, who played in several

---

[7] Beto Guedes, for one, is mentioned forty times by Jonathon Grasse, *The Corner Club* (New York: Bloomsbury, 2020), the 33 1/3 series book on the historic Milton Nascimento et alia LP.

[8] By 1979, Chico had composed at least fifteen song texts in which the voice/narrator/persona is female, whether a lover, spouse, mother, or other role. There are three in the previous drama Chico co-authored with Paulo Pontes, *Gota d'água* (Last straw, 1974), notably the title track. Among the numerous studies of women in Buarque's works, the best is Adélia Bezerra de Meneses, *Figuras do feminino na canção de Chico Buarque* (São Paulo: Ateliê, 2000). She and other observers agree that his grasp of "female psychology" is astounding.

different configurations. The instruments are nylon-string guitar (6 and 7 string), electric guitar, bass, mandolin, *viola* [10–12 steel string folk guitar], *cavaquinho* [akin to a steel-string ukelele], flute, clarinet, trombone, trumpet, alto and tenor sax, drum kit, and the array of percussion: *pandeiro* [tambourine], *cuíca* [friction drum], *surdo* [bass drum], *apito* [whistle], *ganzá*

Figure 3 Chico Buarque and Milton Nascimento in the studio. Photo 1978 by and courtesy of Januário Garcia.

[shaker], *tamborim* [small round frame drum], *repique* [tenor tom tom], *agogô* [double bell], and *caixa* [snare].[9] There is also a conventional string ensemble on four cuts. Among all the musicians credited, some of the more recognizable names— for having made their own records or being first-call studio players—include Raul de Barros on trombone, Chico Batera on traps, Neco on guitar, and the much-in-demand Luizão on bass.[10] Stand-out parts, whether on rhythm tracks or in the interplay of words and music, will be discussed in the course of unpacking the whole album.

[9] English-language print sources to explain the physical specifics and patterns of these Portuguese-named instruments include Larry Crook, *Brazilian Music: Northeastern Traditions and the Heartbeat of a Modern Nation* (Santa Barbara: ABC Clio, 2005), p. 38 ff; and John P. Murphy, *Music in Brazil: Experiencing Music, Expressing Culture* (New York: Oxford U P 2006), p. 10 ff. Internet demonstrations abound.

[10] Luiz de Oliveira da Costa Maia (1949–2005) was tops in his field beginning in the 1970s.

4 Setting the Table, on the Ground

What better way to affirm the out-and-out Brazilian-ness of one's new album than to begin by employing the country's most representative musical genre in a rousing rendition with lyrics about the most typical dish of national cuisine? The opening salvo of the first *Chico Buarque* is such an affirmation: "Feijoada completa" (Complete bean stew meal) serves up on a sound platter an all-embracing black-bean stew repast, i.e. with all the trimmings and side dishes. This A1 track is quite characteristic of the encompassing collection with its sonic frame, crafted lyrics, elements of popular culture, and connections to other genres and dates. It is recreational and didactic alike.

This hungry samba illustrates the vincula with cinema in Chico's oeuvre. It was commissioned by actor-turned-director Hugo Carvana for the film *Se seguru, malandro* (Cool it, hustler) (1978), which was a continuation of his *Vai trabalhar, vagabundo* (Go to work, you bum) (1973).[1] A song of the same

---

[1] I use the English glosses of Randal Johnson and Robert Stam, eds., *Brazilian Cinema*. Expanded edition (New York: Columbia University Press, 1995), p. 407. They use the term "urban hustler" for "the fast-thinking *malandro*." Hugo Carvana is featured in a documentary about his creative processes (available on Youtube): *Como se faz um malandro*. The cited songs appear.

name appears on Chico's 1976 LP *Meus caros amigos*. These cinematic compositions, clearly, belong to the ever-significant *malandro* paradigm in the artist's repertory.

This song depends to a degree on historical conjuncture to be understood fully. In the mid-1970s, the country had entered into a less repressive phase of *distensão* (loosening of tension); people were already beginning to imagine the return of many citizens who had been forced to go abroad or had fled Brazil in fear. Celebrations of the renewal of legality were anticipated. A leading chronicler of Chico's career explains how the request for a film song fit into unfolding public events: the filmmaker asked Chico for "a song for a party that in a certain way would foretell political amnesty and a return to the state of law, banners of struggle of organized social movements. As many mouths were expected at the party—exiles, and, above all, the marginalized people—it was necessary to 'add water to the beans.'"[2] These last words translate *e vamos botar água no feijão,* the folklore-derived refrain of the song text, which is a to-do list and a festive culinary inventory.

Independently, Brazilian health historians viewed "Feijoada completa" as a carol of contented return, noting that it was released in 1978, "the year the Brazilian Amnesty Committee was created, bringing together various civil society organizations" and that it was "teaching the recipe of the most traditional dish of contemporary Brazilian cuisine to welcome returning

[2] Wagner Homem, *Histórias de canções Chico Buarque* (São Paulo: LeYa 2009), p. 111. Jason Stanyek observes that the song comes in the wake of the like-named "Água no feijão" by Jorginho do Império on his 1976 LP *Eu e meu pandeiro.*

political exiles."[3] There are no direct references to current events or political circumstances in the lyric, but they are there, implicit and understood, per the commission of the composition and its interpretation. The words do not really constitute a "recipe" but a series of instructions on what to acquire and prepare. To craft these lines Chico consulted relevant books and precedents, specifically the poem "Feijoada à minha moda" (Bean stew my way) by family friend Vinicius de Moraes, which he dedicated to an author of recipe books he knew.[4] His twenty quatrains consisted of cooking instructions and playful comments about alcohol and food stuffs. More on the words of Chico's song after we consider the two minutes and fifty seconds of the recording.

The arrangement of "Feijoada completa" is an echo and an enactment of the sung narrative. An alert analyst notes that *Chico Buarque* (1978) "begins exactly where *Meus caros amigos* (1976) ends, the song in partnership with Francis Hime, arrangements with flute and arpeggiated piano."[5] That connective tissue is indeed present, but the actual absolute beginning is a plucked guitar figure with *tamborim* syncopating behind it; seconds

---

[3] Francisco de Assis Guedes de Vasconcelos, Mariana Perrelli Vasconcelos, and Iris Helena Guedes de Vasconcelos, "Hunger, Food and Drink in Brazilian Popular Music: A Brief Overview." *História, Ciências, Saúde-Manguinhos*, vol. 22, no. 3 (2015), https://doi.org/10.1590/S0104-59702015000300004. The authors include a full translation of "Feijoada completa."

[4] For Helena Sangirardi. "Feijoada completa" 1962 a poem by Vinicius de Moraes (see his website). Further inter-arts links: the song lyric was rendered in Hungarian by Pál Ferenc, translator of Chico's novel *Budapeste*, and was included—in the voice of Hungarian singers András Domján and Ary Byspo alongside a samba group—in the soundtrack of the film version by Walter Carvalho (2009).

[5] Barros e Silva, *Chico Buarque*, pp. 82–3.

later the piano and a shaker prepare the entry of the voice. The quick instrumental intro is just short of ten seconds. Four stanzas follow, each of close to twenty-five seconds, while the outro is a minute-plus of instrumental iterations of the melody and solos. There is no repetition of the words nor is there a bridge, just four consecutive scenes, as it were, of a gathering depicted. In the first strophe, the voice is mainly backed by the squeaking *cuíca*, *cavaquinho* chords, and bass runs on the seven-string guitar, per the samba genre. These come in just as the voice utters the word "converse," as if the chordophone were an interlocutor. In the first repeat of the form, the voice has a back-and-forth with the flute, an exchange, almost a counterpoint. In the third, the samba whistle is prominent, a call to action, along with the trombone. To close the sung sections, the clarinet has its say along with more hand percussion. Trumpet plays the lead in the instrumental final section, which includes brass and woodwind solos with the whole band. As this dynamic develops, the distribution and entry of instruments can have two figurative senses: they are sprinkled/added on to the plate at the eating affair, and they are joining the fray just as guests come to join to the party.

Twenty years after the release of this song, a young essayist grasped its overall achievement while questioning the arranger's choices: "'Feijoada completa' established the dialectic of domestic malandro-ism under a samba-school arrangement made corny by the wind instruments (an evil that spreads through the record)."[6] As will be seen in the discussion

---

[6] Pedro Alexandre Sanches, *Tropicalismo: decadência bonita do samba* (São Paulo: Boitempo, 2000), p. 228.

of the text below, the relational attribution is quite apt, but the impression of the sonic dimension may be a bit out of tune. While it is accurate that most of the instruments of a *carnaval* samba school are employed here, the particular blending of rhythmic parts and brass-flute-clarinet is actually more like a stage band at a *gafieira*, one of Rio de Janeiro's old-time integrated dance halls. True, that space is inside, nocturnal and likely more crowded than the backyard gig in the song, but it is hardly a drawback. Others might hear echoes of the *choro* genre, Brazil's equivalent of ragtime-early jazz, which is the musical mold of the bridge song "Meu caro amigo."[7]

The 1994 box set of select Chico songs includes "Feijoada completa" on the disc *O cronista*, the chronicler or author of *crônicas*, the most widely consumed genre of Brazilian literature. A *crônica* is a short prose piece usually appearing as a column in a periodical publication (newspaper, magazine, more recently internet) and concerning some aspect of modern life or social situation. It can range from humorous or poetic meandering to moving narratives or sociological commentary. The *crônica*-like "Feijoada completa" sings of groceries and human situations.[8] There are four sextains, each introduced by the word *mulher*, woman and wife, whom the narrator addresses throughout. Each strophe ends with a first-person plural command to add water to the beans, i.e. increase

[7] There is a good study in English, Tamara Elena Livingston-Isenhour and Thomas George Caracas Garcia, *Choro: A Social History of a Brazilian Popular Music* (Bloomington: Indiana U P, 2005).

[8] Fiction writer and *cronista* Luiz Fernando Verissimo (1936) wrote a 2010 story intitled "Feijoada completa'" which in turn had a short film adaptation (2012) by Angelo Defanti.

the volume of food for the guests. In the first strophe, the man announces that he has invited some friends over to chat and lots of cold beer is in order, *cerveja estupidamente gelada prum batalhão* (stupidly chilled beer for a batallion). The second elicits Brazil's typical sugarcane rum (*cachaça*) and sausage, noting that there is no need to set the table, folks can sit on the floor/ground. In the third and fourth stanzas, he tells her what to cook, put out, or add to the cauldron: crisp pork rinds, white rice, manioc flour with toppings, peppers, oranges, pork sausage, jerky, gravy, collard greens, i.e. the complete package. All is wrapped up when he tells her to allege lack of funds and pass on financial responsibility to someone else. The going-out phrase—*diz que tá dura, pendura a fatura no nosso irmão* (say you're broke, stick our brother with the bill)—is ripe for construal, usually targeting the military regime but also possibly alluding to the International Monetary Fund, with which Brazil has some history.

This song has elicited a good deal of reaction and comment from many different fields: musicology, history, political science, sociology, literature, journalism, geography, gender studies, and the open-ended opinion venues of the ever-burgeoning internet. As there is a focus on food and drink, it makes sense to concede a basic principle of enjoyment in play. One youthful analyst stresses that what is at stake in the song is "confraternization among friends; it shows, step by step, in a simple and fun setting, how easy it is to install an atmosphere of the purest pleasure."[9] What is more diverting

---

[9] Fabiane Batista Pinto, "O Brasil de Chico Buarque: nação memória e povo." Master's Thesis in Sociology. Federal University of Ceará. Fortaleza, Ceará, 2007. p. 73.

than a backyard barbecue with the whole gang, surely with live music, on a Sunday afternoon? It bears noting that the word *feijoada*, by metonymy or association, may also signify the gathering of eaters itself, a socializing thing. One blogger smartly notes—beyond the jocose tone, the air of hospitality, the commanding character of the Brazilian man at home, the assumed servility of the woman, and her inability to object— how the feel of percussive words about the rounds of rum— *uca, açúcar, cumbuca de gelo, limão*—also suggest round samba itself.[10] Airs of patriarchy, sexism, even misogyny, are an integral part of the portrait of the narrator. The extensive web chatter about "Feijoada completa" often refers to the "friends" as those returning from exile. One should also consider the evocation of endemic social problems, hunger, and thirst in a literal sense in a land with high rates of poverty and undernourishment, in addition to the figuration of political deprivation and a desire for amelioration. While the macho character of the narrator, easy to peg as a variety of malandro at home, and his embodiment of individual machismo, are undeniable themes, a collective ethos still emerges. In terms of musical history, Chico's song joins a decades-long list of sambas expressing masculine domination.

When the tune has concluded—when all are seated and the brew and stew are complete(d)—the *festa popular*, the party of the people, has come to fruition. There is an opening for all. A caring journalist wraps up his evaluation of "Feijoada completa" as a "miracle of simplicity, a genuine roots samba,

10 https://outraspalavras.net/mauricioayer/chico-buarque-e-a-cachaca-1-o-trabalhador-em-festa/ Molhando a palavra: literatura e cachaça com Mauricio Ayer Posted 7/30/2020.

yet ingenious." The occasion has wide, multi-class resonance: it brought forth "in the most characteristic and joyful way possible a Brazil that was muffled, missing, forgotten not just by the dictatorship but by organized civil society that fed on the 'smart songs' as it practiced resistance." The friends are not just university types but the common folk, "last minute guests

Figure 4 Chico Buarque, *c*. 1980, photo by Marisa Alvarez Lima, courtesy of Marisco Editora Musical.

at the democratic banquet."[11] The invitations, the acceptances, the arrivals, the participations, the sharing, the giving of thanks, all is made to happen in words and music in a characteristically unified Chico Buarquean manner.

---

[11] Barros e Silva, *Chico Buarque*, pp. 82–3.

Feijoada completa (Buarque)

Mulher
Você vai gostar
Tô levando uns amigos pra conversar
Eles vão com uma fome que nem me contem
Eles vão com uma sede de anteontem
Salta cerveja estupidamente gelada prum batalhão
E vamos botar água no feijão
Mulher
Não vá se afobar
Não tem que pôr a mesa, nem dá lugar
Ponha os pratos no chão, e o chão 'tá posto
E prepare as lingüiças pro tiragosto
Uca, açúcar, cumbuca de gelo, limão
E vamos botar água no feijão
Mulher
Você vai fritar
Um montão de torresmo pra acompanhar
Arroz branco, farofa e a malagueta
A laranja-bahia ou da seleta
Joga o paio, carne-seca, toucinho no caldeirão
E vamos botar água no feijão
Mulher
Depois de salgar
Faça um bom refogado, que é pra engrossar
Aproveite a gordura da frigideira
Pra melhor temperar a couve mineira
Diz que 'tá dura, pendura a fatura no nosso irmão
E vamos botar água no feijão.

© Editora Musical Cara Nova, 1977; now administered by Marola Edições Musicais.

Complete Bean Stew Meal

Woman
You're gonna like this
I'm bringing some friends over for a chat
They're so hungry, don't even tell me about it
Their thirst is like from the day before yesterday
Bring out the super frosty beer for a battalion
And let's add some water to the bean stew!
Woman
Don't go getting flustered
You don't have to set the table, ain't even enough places
Just set the dishes on the ground, 'cuz the floor's ready
And prepare the sausages as appetizers
Cane rum, sugar, ice bucket, lemons
And let's add some water to the bean stew!
Woman
You're gonna fry
A bunch of pork rinds as a side dish
White rice, cassava flour and hot peppers
Bahia oranges or the select type
Toss the dried sausage, jerky, bacon in the cauldron
And let's add some water to the bean stew!
Woman
After adding salt
Cook well to thicken the broth
Use the fat from the frying pan
Better to season the Minas-style collard greens
Say you're broke and stick our brother with the bill
And let's add some water to the bean stew!

5 Spelling Out a Partnership in Rhyme

The dear friends Francis Hime and Chico Buarque enjoyed a fruitful musico-poetic partnership for twelve years, 1972–84. They teamed up for two tracks on the latter's 1978 LP: "Trocando em miudos" (Spelling things out) and "Pivete" (Lil' hood), a sharp pair of compositions that illustrate, respectively, the affective and urban social sensibilities of Chico the poet of song, and the skills of Mr. Hime as composer-arranger-conductor. They are the third tracks on the A and B sides of the album, an appreciable, if most likely coincidental, order. Both songs have had lives independent of the release of the first *Chico Buarque*.

The invited lyricist set the music to words that provided the name "Trocando em miudos" for a nifty break-up ballad. Hime had determined the melody and harmony beforehand and given them to Chico for him to write words.[1] That is the preferred operational method when composer and wordsmith

---

[1] As the story goes, Hime was all set to record the tune with a working title when the better-late-than-never Chico showed up in the studio at the eleventh hour with words and a title. A photo of his manuscript is included in Joana Levenroth Hime, "Uma biografia a dois (Francis e Francisco) 12 anos de parceria." MA thesis, PUC-Rio de Janeiro, 2016. See www.francishime.com. br for other data.

partner on a tune. Hime's instrument is piano, where he usually creates, but in this instance he forged the sound design on the guitar.[2] The title is included in vol. 2 of Almir Chediak's *Songbook Bossa Nova* and was first recorded on Hime's LP *Passaredo* (Flock of birds, 1977), with a fundamentally bossa-nova feel, although the composer's own score indicates *samba-canção*, the bolero-like lyrical variant of samba most popular in the 1950s. On the first *Chico Buarque*, things are somewhat different. There is no clear underlying bossa or *samba-canção*, in fact there are no drums or percussion, nor bass. The auditory dimension is all flutes, piano and string ensemble to back the voice. In terms of genre, one could call this version just plain *canção* (song). However it might be categorized, the performance is absorbing.

Interplay of words and music is effective in Chico's rendition. The structure is simple, eight-bar flute statements open and close. There are three consecutive 18-measure verses, each with a distinct final four bars, a detail that can be heard to affect reception. If the prelude with teary flutes seems to be suggesting that a somber story is on the way, the flute-led afterword would be saying "and now you've heard my sad tale." The text can be divided into three sets of eight lines with double end-rhymes in each, but there are variations. The verses begin and proceed in major tonality in a more affirmative fashion, while the minor modulation that follows is for more painful utterances. The first verse has an "extra" prosodic line (9 not 8). The second verse has a noticeable melodic jump at the end, where the most intense words fall, and different chords.

---

[2] Interview with Francis Hime, *Correio Braziliense* on line November 26, 2017.

The third verse is introduced by an interjection and pause, and does not resolve back to the major tonic. This lack of precise symmetry among the verses is a subtle reflection of the mildly disturbed mindset of the narrator.

Asked to discuss this sung fiction, Chico reminisces about the tragic samba-songs of the 1950s associated with *dor-de-cotovelo*, elbow pain caused by leaning too hard on bended arm while drowning one's sorrows at the bar and bemoaning romantic troubles, especially end-of-relationship goodbyes. The most severe ones were *rasga coração*, ripping the heart. The context of the 1970s, with women's liberation already happening, makes breakups a bit easier (Chico's nod to more equal rights?), but still tough.[3] The song title, and key line, is a Brazilian Portuguese idiomatic expression; the literal meaning of the words is changing into little pieces (of rendered animals or monetary coins); the effective meaning is to explain, clarify, and spell out. In the lyric, all the things the male narrator points to come after a downer of a point of departure: the domestic life with the woman he addresses is over and done with. He begins by telling her that he will leave the folk ribbon from Bahia, a supposed charm that did him no good, but he will keep the record by Pixinguinha, the Brazilian equivalent of Louis Armstrong (there is a famous 1957 photo of the two when the latter visited Brazil); everything else is hers. In other words: she can put away or forget what's left of all that one calls home, the shadows of what they were, the love stains on their sheets, their best memories, the hope that they would

---

[3] DVD *Chico Buarque: ROMANCE* (EMI Universal, 2006), spoken presentation before recorded performance of the song.

work everything out, the ring that's now just for pawning or melting down. He won't give her the pleasure of seeing him weep nor charge her for the damage done to his heart, but he'll offer a little something for her next love and the rent. He asks for her to return the Neruda (a book of poetry by the feted Chilean poet) that she did not even read. He'll go out the door with his ID, one for the road, much *saudade* (longing imbued with memory), and the impression that it was, after all, high time. The similarity of some words in the original adds to a sense of cohesion in the singer's discourse of distress.

Much is made of the unusual feminine perspective in Chico's lyrical universe, but the masculine experience is also poeticized frequently. "Feelings of despair involved in separation, of course, are not exclusive to songs written from a woman's point of view, [they are] a prominent characteristic of Buarque's poetics."[4] In "Trocando em miudos" what is most effective is the transference of emotion to objects, possessions, signs of affection; these are the *miudos*, the little things that prove to mean so much and have an explanatory element.

One might think that this song is pure lament in the love department. But there are related extra-amatory incidents to mention. A local poet reported that censors were suspicious of this song text when it was submitted for approval because, one assumes, it was by their nemesis Chico Buarque, and more specifically because it mentioned Pablo Neruda, known to be

[4] Luciana C. Monteiro, "Cross-dressed Poetics: Lessons and Limits of Gender Transgression in Brazilian Popular Music." MA Thesis, University of Florida, 2007, p. 37, citing examples of compositions that reflected men's profound suffering identified by Maria Helena Sansão Fontes, *Sem fantasia: masculino- feminino em Chico Buarque* (Rio de Janeiro: Graphia, 2003).

Trocando em miudos (Hime-Buarque)

Eu vou lhe deixar a medida do Bonfim
Não me valeu
Mas fico com o disco do Pixinguinha, sim?
O resto é seu
Trocando em miudos, pode guardar
As sobras de tudo que chamam lar
As sombras de tudo que fomos nós
As marcas de amor nos nossos lençóis
As nossas melhores lembranças
Aquela esperança de tudo se ajeitar
Pode esquecer
Aquela aliança, você pode empenhar
Ou derreter
Mas devo dizer que não vou lhe dar
O enorme prazer de me ver chorar
Nem vou lhe cobrar pelo seu estrago
Meu peito tão dilacerado
Aliás
Aceite uma ajuda do seu futuro amor
Pro aluguel
Devolva o Neruda que você me tomou
E nunca leu
Eu bato o portão sem fazer alarde
Eu levo a carteira de identidade
Uma saideira, muita saudade
E a leve impressão de que já vou tarde

© 1977 by Editora Musical Cara Nova Ltda. Now controlled by Marola Edições Musicais.

Spelling things out

I'll leave the Bonfim ribbon for you
It didn't me do me any good
But the Pixinguinha record stays with me, OK?
Everything else is yours
Spelling things out, you can keep
The leftovers of all they call home
The shadows of everything we were
The stains of love on our sheets
Our very best memories
That hope that everything would work out
You can forget about it
That wedding band, you can pawn it
Or even melt it down
But I must say that I will not give you
The great pleasure of seeing me weep
Nor will I charge you for damage done
My breast so torn to pieces
By the way
Here's a little something for your next love
To help pay the rent
Return that Neruda of mine that you took
But never read
I'll slam the gate without too much fuss
I'll take my identification card
One last drink for the road, so much yearning
I 've got the slight impression that it's high time

a member of the Chilean Communist Party. Chico supposedly instructed his lawyers to tell the censorship bureau not to worry because in the narrative of the song the woman did not even read the book. The song was approved without modifications.[5] Chico does not have a clear recollection of this episode, but the mere fact that such a story would circulate is indicative of the unrelenting irritation he had to deal with because of military censors. Further to the overall impact of the song, one academic interpretation alleges that "Trocando em miudos" can be discussed under the guise of "double meanings."[6] It is not so far from the political tenor of "Apesar de você" (Chapter 10): the voice lamenting separation from his lover wants his Neruda book back (political symbolism?) and the Pixinguinha record (popular preference?). There is, as in protest tunes, a rejection of what happened and a disposition for a better life.

Like "Feijoada completa," the lively song "Pivete" falls under the rubric *cronista* in the 1994 box set. With Hime's woodwind-led orchestration of an urban soundscape in a samba frame, Chico's peripatetic lyric "chronicles" the comings and goings of a *pivete*—a child thief, a boy working for an adult criminal, a juvenile delinquent, or a street waif—of which there are plenty in Rio de Janeiro. Truth be told, this song ought to be in those books that bring together songs about or set in the

---

[5] Homem, *Historias de canções*, p. 125.

[6] Renato Janine Ribeiro, "A utopia lírica de Chico Buarque de Hollanda." In Berenice Cavalcante et al, eds. *Decantando a República: inventário histórico e político da canção popular moderna brasileira*, vol. 1 (Rio de Janeiro: Nova Fronteira, 2004), p. 160.

"Marvelous City."[7] What is notable about the tune "Pivete" is that the composition was finished just before being taken into the studio. The makers of the album realized at a certain point in advance of the taping sessions that there was insufficient material for a standard size LP (10–12 tracks, 30-ish minutes), so the feature artist and his main music man came to the rescue (more on this in Chapter 7). Given Chico's known interest in both social conditions and children's issues, it is not a stretch to assert that the idea for such a song was already spinning around his head. Chico would have had some parts figured out but it was not fully ready when recording dates were to begin. It would be up to Hime to create and complement the musical mold for the founding notions. The result was sufficiently satisfying that *Pivete* was originally proposed as the title of the album.[8] Together with the bright flutes, what stands out is the active bass line (courtesy of the renowned Luizão), which moves like a brisk truck through traffic.

The melody is rather simple, basically one extended and repetitive motif. The lines of the rhymed text are short (3–4 words) and replete with street slang, perchance a bit "complicated" for unaccustomed ears but a gold mine for a sociolinguist. The narration is composed of the adventures of a transgressive kid who sells gum, wipes cars with a rag,

---

[7] For example, Marcelo Moutinho, *Cançoes do Rio a cidade em letra e música* (Rio de Janeiro: Casa da Palavra, 2010). Cf. Rafaela Gambarra, *Turismo musical no Rio de Janeiro* (Lisbon: Chiado, 2018), a tour of the city entirely based on songs by Chico Buarque. When the publication of the Americas Society in New York did a special issue on Rio and Bahia, they commissioned my translation of this song, as the guest editors felt that "Pivete" was a worthy sign of carioca life. *Review: Literature and Arts of the Americas*, no. 83 (November 2011).

[8] J. Hime, p. 83.

Pivete (Hime-Buarque)

No sinal fechado
Ele vende chiclete
Capricha na flanela
E se chama Pelé
Pinta na janela
Batalha algum trocado
Aponta um canivete
E até
Dobra a Carioca, olerê
Desce a Frei Caneca, olará
Se manda pra Tijuca
Sobe o Borel
Meio se maloca
Agita numa boca
Descola uma mutuca
E um papel
Sonha aquela mina, olerê
Prancha, parafina, olará
Dorme gente fina
Acorda pinel
Zanza na sarjeta
Fatura uma besteira
E tem as pernas tortas
E se chama Mané
Arromba uma porta
Faz ligação direta
Engata uma primeira
E até
Dobra a Carioca, olerê
Desce a Frei Caneca, olará
Se manda pra Tijuca

Lil' Hood'

At the red light
He sells chewing gum
Does his best with a rag
And he's called Pele
He pops up at the window
Battles to get a little change
Pulls a jackknife
And later!
He turns onto Carioca Lane, oh-lay-ray
Goes down Frei Caneca Way, oh-lah-rah
Takes off for Tijuca town
Goes up Borel Hill
He crouches and slinks
Moves around a point
Scores a lid
And some papers
He dreams about that chick, oh-lay-ray
A board, some wax, oh-lah-rah
Goes to sleep in nice shape
Wakes up flipped out
He wanders down the street
Makes next to nothing
And he's bow-legged
And he's called Manny
He breaks into a car
Connects a hot wire
Puts it in first gear
And later!
He turns onto Carioca Lane, oh-lay-ray
Goes down Frei Caneca Way, oh-lah-rah
Takes off for Tijuca town

Na contramão
Dança para-lama
Já era para-choque
Agora ele se chama
Emersão (Ayrtão, 1993)
Sobe no passeio, olerê
Pega no Recreio, olará
Não se liga em freio
Nem direção
No sinal fechado
Ele transa chiclete
E se chama pivete
E pinta na janela
Capricha na flanela
Descola uma bereta
Batalha na sarjeta
E tem as pernas tortas

1978 © by Trevo Editora Musical, now controlled by Marola
Edições Musicais.

Goin' the wrong way
Last dance of the fenders
The bumpers are done with
Now he's called
Emerson (Big Ayrton, 1993)
He goes up the overpass, oh-lay-ray
Down toward Recreio, oh-lah-rah
He pays the brakes no mind
Nor the steering
At the red light
He does the gum thing
And he's called lil' hood'
And he pops up at the window
He does his best with the rag
He gets himself a Beretta
Battles to get ahead in the street
And he's bow-legged

and begs, with a jackknife, at the stop light, and darts around locations in the city. His crimes include drug use, hot wiring a car, and bad driving. In his mind there are popular sports heroes: soccer legends Pelé and Mané (Garrincha) and Formula One race-car driver Emerson (Fittipaldi), which changes in the second life of the song.

Chico later read a story about street kinds in downtown Rio who would beg in a mixture of languages; so he made an addition.[9] When he published his lyrics in book form, the page for "Pivete" now featured an epigraph: "Monsieur have money per mangiare." In turn, he used this phrase on the re-recording on the album *Paratodos* (For all) (1993), the cover of which includes a mug shot of Chico from when he was arrested as a teen for vehicle theft. In the new version, the race-car driver mentioned has changed to Ayrton (Senna), a more recent hero of the Brazilian masses. Sadly, a massacre of street kids took place in 1993 at the site about which Chico had read; quite a macabre contrast with the upbeat-despite-indigent tone of the song "Pivete."

[9] Homem, *Historias de cancoes*, p. 124. Cf. Chico Buarque, *Letra e música* (São Paulo: Companhia das Letras, 1989), p. 172.

6 A Trio of Stage Tunes

From the late 1960s to the late 1970s, Chico Buarque distinguished himself as a playwright, an author of musicals who wrote dramatic verse and integrated songs.[1] The best of these can be powerful stand-alone numbers; such is the case with the three compositions from *Ópera do malandro* included on the first *Chico Buarque:* "O meu amor," "Pedaço de mim," and "Homenagem ao malandro." The musical had already opened when Chico and crew recorded the 1978 LP, so theatre-goers were already familiar, but for most of the listening public these were fresh sounds. A year later all of the eighteen songs in the theatre production would comprise a double LP for the artist, and in the mid-1980s Chico would write a couple of additional items for the film version. In 1978, the three select songs were showcases for vocal talent, compelling emotion, and sociohistorical irony.

"O meu amor" is a bolero, a Spanish-American genre that was practiced in Rio de Janeiro in the 1940s, the temporal setting of the opera. Francis Hime's arrangement uses string ensemble, woodwinds, brass and percussion; as on another track, the bass of Luizão is solid and commanding. But the feature is the vocal duet, the sing-off of two female characters

---

[1] On these efforts, see Charles A. Perrone, "Dissonance and Dissent: The Musical Dramatics of Chico Buarque." *Latin American Theater Review*, vol. 22, no. 2 (1989), pp. 81–94.

vying for a man. Their words are sensual, about the pleasures he gives them. For censors to permit the recording, the most explicit words had to be changed, but the sexy mood remains. The first lady says that his unique way of doing things drives her hair-raising crazy, that his kisses reach her very soul. The second counters that he steals her senses and violates her ears with indecent secrets and navel-bound teeth. Together they sing the refrain: *Eu sou sua menina, viu?/E ele é o meu rapaz/Meu corpo é testemunha/Do bem que ele me faz* (I am his girl, hear?/ and he is my guy/my body is witness/to the good that he does me). Round two has neck caresses and thighs between thighs vs. frontal kissing and making himself at home. Bodily imagery, clearly, is the name of the game. Even tamed, the song was banned from radio broadcast. But it made quite an impression in any case.

Brazil's most eloquent music critic concluded an analysis of the MPB of the 1970s with these insights about the trend's most prominent figure:

> Chico Buarque, a most able artisan, reads what people have on the inside: his dramatic lyric is extremely sensitive to the body that suffers and feels pleasure. His poetry-music is full of images of hurting and corporeal intensity: he captures *visceral feeling*, and for this reason he is so fine for the *erotic*, the *social* (reading the future as it is inscribed in the viscera that suffer) and the *feminine*. [original emphasis][2]

---

[2] Wisnik, *Sem receita*, p. 189. The segment cited here in *Sem receita* is a reprint of a chapter in *Anos 70—música popular* (1979), a series of pocket books on each of the arts in the decade, under the sign of dictatorship, with censorship having been mollified as of late 1978.

Nowhere are these words better suited than in "O meu amor" and the sister song "Pedaço de mim," also a duet but this time a he-and-she situation of separation, at the termination of a passionate affair. No genre is identified for "Pedaço de mim," but one could list it as popular vocal chamber music, or even as *modinha* (little sentimental song), the dominant mode of Luso-Brazilian song from the mid-nineteenth century until *c.* 1930. In any case it is intense and dramatic, both literally, as part of the work of theatre, and figuratively, as a gripping piece of poetic music. The arrangement by Milton Nascimento is not elaborate (acoustic guitar + bass, piano, mandolin) but just right for the dark chord patterns. In the middle of the deliberate song, the female voice does backing vocables that are haunting. She (Zizi Possi) sings strophes one and three, while He (Chico) does two and four, and the last stanza is two-part harmony. The melody does not change verse to verse nor does it include any surprising intervals, though it is perfectly married to the words and beguiling in itself.

The text is built on parallelism and shared elements, all about the pain of separation. Each division has the title words, the word *metade* (half, as in "better half"), the imperative "take away," and the noun *saudade,* a quintessential notion of the Luso-Brazilian imaginary since the inception of sung poetry in Medieval times. The term incorporates missing, nostalgia, yearning, fond remembrance, and has been nicely rendered as "memory imbued with longing" (James L. Taylor, *A Portuguese-English Dictionary*, 1958). Like *malandro*, the word *saudade* is best used as a borrowed term, which may not always be feasible. In each sextain the title words are a vocative, as is the modified suffering *half* (removed, exiled, torn off, amputated, adored). The five figurations of *saudade* are rather strong: one refers to a dead child, another to a lost member. It is, at the end, the worst punishment.

This composition has dazzled analysts across disciplines. Musicologist and semiotician Luiz Tatit wrote that it attained "an unaccustomed level of sophistication in Brazilian song," underlining the tight relationship of words and music: with an unchanging melodic grid, "the metaphorical precision of the strophes make the opposing energies—coming close/drawing away—palpitate," and "all of the textual thrusts go the way of shaping the nucleus of passion for the maximum yield of melodic tensions."[3] Not only is "Pedaço de mim" a technical masterpiece, it assumed a role in current events. The "disjunctive content of the song" was incorporated by the campaign for amnesty, by all indications with the composer's support, becoming "one of the most pungent manifestos of the day" and actually "amplified the calls for amnesty for the victims of the authoritarian regime."[4]

Historian Marcos Napolitano considers "Pedaço de mim" to be paradigmatic of an alternate kind of *abertura* song, a cluster giving "heroic and sublime meaning to the experience of the leaden years." The "poetic-musical climate of these songs was darker, melancholy, and tension prevailed, opposed by a movement to overcome the collective traumas generated by the circle of fear as imposed on the most critical sectors of

---

[3] Luiz Tatit, *O cancionista: composição de canções no Brasil* (São Paulo: EDUSP, 1996), pp. 239, 241.

[4] Tatit, *Cancionista*, p. 241; Luiz Tatit, "Tensões da dor." In Rinaldo Fernandes, ed. *Chico Buarque do Brasil: textos sobre as canções, o teatro, e a ficção de um artista brasileiro* (Rio de Janeiro: Editora Garamond, 2004), p. 305.

society."[5] Countless Brazilians were separated from loved ones due to imprisonments, exiles, torture, and death; thus the relevance and invocation of this song outside its theatrical and popular-music contexts. Napolitano detects mourning and melancholy in the song, as well as temporal and existential threats "lived under the sign of irreplaceable loss provoked by an epoch of extreme oppression."[6]

Since 1980, the foremost author in textual criticism about Chico Buarque has been Adélia Bezerra de Meneses, who never fails to express admiration for the poet-musician's grasp of women's vantages. "Pedaço de mim," in particular, is seen to reveal "the state of incompleteness and absence, and the consequent feeling of mutilation impelled by separation." This applies to the masculine point of view too, but "the feminine feeling of loss, of privation and absence comes forth with enormous strength."[7] Even more grandiose are the psychological and mythical components in the fabric of Chico's song of separation:

> ... here there is a convergence of elements: from a psychoanalytic perspective, the castration complex, the feminine perception that a piece is missing, as Freud desired; from the perspective of myth, there is a dual reference. On

---

[5] Marcos Napolitano, "Brazilian Popular Music: The Soundtrack of the Political Opening (1975/1982)." *Estudos avançados*, vol. 24, no. 69 (2010), p. 395. Original English.

[6] Marcos Napolitano, "Hoje preciso refletir um pouco: ser social e e tempo histórico na obra de Chico Buarque de Hollanda 1971/1978." *História São Paulo*, vol. 22, no. 1 (2003), p. 131.

[7] Adélia Bezerra de Meneses, "Chico Buarque: The Creator and the Revelator." In Chediak, vol. 2, pp. 19 and 26.

Pedaço de mim (Buarque)

Ela:
Oh, pedaço de mim
Oh, metade afastada de mim
Leva o teu olhar
Que a saudade é o pior tormento
É pior do que o esquecimento
É pior do que se entrevar
Ele:
Oh, pedaço de mim
Oh, metade exilada de mim
Leva os teus sinais
Que a saudade dói como um barco
Que aos poucos descreve um arco
E evita atracar no cais
Ela:
Oh, pedaço de mim
Oh, metade arrancada de mim
Leva o vulto teu
Que a saudade é o revés de um parto
A saudade é arrumar o quarto
Do filho que já morreu
Ele:
Oh, pedaço de mim
Oh, metade amputada de mim
Leva o que há de ti
Que a saudade dói latejada
É assim como uma fisgada
No membro que já perdi
Ela e Ele:
Oh, pedaço de mim
Oh, metade adorada de mim

Piece of me

She:
Oh dear piece of me,
Oh dear half disaffected from me
Take away your gaze,
For longing in loss is the worst torment
It is worse than being forgotten
It is worse than being left crippled
He:
Oh dear piece of me,
Oh dear half exiled from me
Take away your beauty spots
For longing in loss hurts like a ship
That bit by bit traces an arc
Yet avoids docking in the harbor
She:
Oh dear piece of me,
Oh dear half torn from me
Take away your shape and figure
For longing in loss is childbirth in reverse
Longing in loss is to tidy up the room
of a son who has already died
He:
Oh dear piece of me,
Oh dear half amputated from me
Take away what there is of you
For longing in loss is throbbing pain
It is like a sharp twinge
in the member that I have lost
She and He:
Oh dear piece of me,
Oh dear half worshipped in me

Leva os olhos meus
Que a saudade é o pior castigo
E eu não quero levar comigo
A mortalha do amor
Adeus

© 1977, Marola Edições Musicais.

O meu amor (Buarque)

Teresinha:
O meu amor
Tem um jeito manso que é só seu
E que me deixa louca
Quando me beija a boca
A minha pele toda fica arrepiada
E me beija com calma e fundo
Até minh'alma se sentir beijada, ai
Lúcia:
O meu amor
Tem um jeito manso que é só seu
Que rouba os meus sentidos
Viola os meus ouvidos
Com tantos segredos lindos e indecentes
Depois brinca comigo
Ri do meu umbigo
E me crava os dentes, ai
As duas:
Eu sou sua menina, viu?
E ele é o meu rapaz
Meu corpo é testemunha
Do bem que ele me faz

Wash all away from my eyes
For longing in loss is the worst punishment
And I don't want to carry with me
The shroud of love
Farewell.

My love

Teresinha:
My love
has a gentle way that is his alone
and that drives me crazy
when he kisses my lips
all my skin is left shivering
And he kisses me with calm and depth
until my very soul feels kissed, oh
Lúcia:
My love
has a gentle way that is his alone
that steals my senses
violates my ears
with so many lovely and indecent secrets
then he plays with me
laughs at my belly button
and sinks his teeth into me, oh
T & L:
I'm his girl, see?
And he's my man
My body is witness
to the good he does me

Lúcia:

O meu amor

Tem um jeito manso que é só seu

De me deixar maluca

Quando me roça a nuca

E quase me machuca com a barba mal feita

E de pousar as coxas entre as minhas coxas

Quando ele se deita, ai

Teresinha:

O meu amor

Tem um jeito manso que é só seu

De me fazer rodeios

De me beijar os seios

Me beijar o ventre

E me deixar em brasa

Desfruta do meu corpo

Como se o meu corpo fosse a sua casa, ai

As duas:

Eu sou sua menina, viu?

E ele é o meu rapaz

Meu corpo é testemunha

Do bem que ele me faz

Lúcia:
My love
has a gentle way that is his alone
of driving me crazy
when he strokes my neck and
almost hurts me with his unshaven whiskers
and placing his thighs between my own
when he lies down, oh
Teresinha:
My love
has a gentle way that is his alone
of hemming and hawing on me
of kissing these breasts of mine
kissing my belly
and leaving me in embers
He enjoys my body
as if my body were his home, oh
T & L:
I'm his girl, see?
And he's my man.
My body is witness
to the good he does me.

one hand, an allusion to the Androgyne in Plato's *Banquet*: the composed being, divided by Zeus into two halves, that will search for each other, inescapably, for the rest of their lives … On the other hand, still on the mythical plane, but in a different cultural strain, there is an allusion to the narration of the Creation of Man, as in Genesis, the first book of the Bible: the creation of Eve, by Yaweh, from one of Adam's ribs.[8]

In sum, there is quite a bit going on in "Pedaço de mim." It can be appreciated for its place in a play, intense vocals, productive melody, poignant harmonic atmosphere, and exquisite text with reverberations in an anguished here-and-now, plus way beyond 1978, and as distant as the origins of the species.

The 1978 track most clearly related to *Ópera do malandro* is "Homenagem ao malandro," one of three framing songs for the play. The lead number "O malandro"—a version of "Die Moritat Von Mackie Messer" (Kurt Weill-Bertolt Brecht) ("Mack the Knife")—constitutes a first prologue; a final version of the same (Nº 2) serves as epilogue, following the "happy end." Chico's original, precedes the second act, and, closes side A of the first *Chico Buarque*, as a sort of halfway marker, an older style samba in between the two modern sambas that are the first and last tracks on the album. The arrangements of the three tracks reflect the contrast; the 1940s-esque woodwinds in the homage are the clearest indicator.

---

[8] Adélia Bezerra de Meneses, "Dois guris–ou a maternidade ferida." In Rinaldo Fernandes, ed. *Chico Buarque: o poeta das mulheres, dos desvalidos e dos perseguidos: ensaios sobre a mulher, o pobre e a repressão militar nas canções de Chico* (São Paulo: LeYa, 2013), p. 20.

This middle song depicts the demise of the classic *malandro* of Rio de Janeiro and suggests that the tradition of malandro-ism—*malandragem*—hustling, deception, and getting around the law, as opposed to working honestly— moved up the social ladder. The narrator set out to pay homage to the cream of the crop of malandros from times past, but he wasted a trip to their usual neighborhood in Rio because such no longer exists. Now there's an abnormal number of regular, professional rogues, with official swank, candidates for federal malandro, in social columns, with contracts, ties, capital, who never go wrong. The real malandro put his knife down to have a wife and kids and things; he might even be working and take the train into town. End of verses. From them we gather that now (late 1940s in the play) the malandro is not a Bohemian shark but someone in the system, employed, elected, maybe leading some business. This would constitute a comment on corruption during the advance of consumer capitalism mid-century and, by extension, in the 1970s. Exemplified in "Homenagem ao malandro," the character and social type seen from different temporal angles is a way for Chico to ponder historical contrast:

> The figure of the malandro ... is an attempt to affirm that problematic space of tension between the old and the new, the past and the present, the apogee and decadence, cordiality and brutality, in the gallery of his carioca human personages.[9]

9 Julio Dinis, "Chico Buarque—meu falso mentiroso." In Sylvia Cyntrão, ed. *Chico Buarque, sinal aberto* (Rio de Janeiro: 7 Letras, 2015), p. 196.

A Trio of Stage Tunes

Homenagem ao malandro (Buarque)

Eu fui fazer um samba em homenagem
à nata da malandragem
que eu conheço de outros carnavais
Eu fui à Lapa e perdi a viagem
Que aquela tal malandragem
não existe mais
Agora já não é normal
o que dá de malandro regular profissional
Malandro com aparato de malandro oficial
Malandro candidato a malandro federal
Malandro com retrato na coluna social
Malandro com contrato com gravata e capital
que nunca se dá mal
Mas o malandro pra valer
—não espalha
Aposentou a navalha
Tem mulher e filho e tralha e tal
Dizem as más línguas que ele até trabalha
Mora lá longe e chacoalha
num trem da Central

© 1978 Marola Edições Musicais

Homage to the malandro

I set out to write a samba-homage
to the choicest malandros
That I know from *carnaval* years ago
I went to their part of town but the trip was a waste
since that kind of malandro-ism
no longer exists
And now it's not normal
How many regular, professional malandros there are
Malandro with the pomp of an official malandro
Malandro candidate for federal malandro
Malandro with his picture in the society column
Malandro with contracts, a tie, and capital
For whom nothing ever goes wrong
But the real-deal malandro
—don't spread the word—
put his knife down
He has a wife and kids and stuff
Nasty rumor is that he might even be working
He lives quite a way from here,
and takes the Central Line train

The malandro can take many different turns in Chico's late-seventies musical domain, and, the last track of the A side having been spun, we can turn the 33 1/3 over on the turntable (or, OK, just let the CD or list of digital files keep playing) to hear one other variant of malandro on the very first track of the side B.

Figure 5   Chico Buarque, *c.* 1980 photo by Marisa Alvarez Lima courtesy of Marisco Editora Musical.

7 A Loose Can(n)on

The second side of the first *Chico Buarque* opens with "Até o fim" (Until the end), a novelty tune in which there is a lot more going on than it might seem at first sight and listen. In the 1994 box set this composition is included on the *malandro* disc, and the persona of the lyric is indeed a down-on-his-luck ne'er-do-well who is nevertheless persistent, a loose cannon of sorts. The point of departure for the song text is the Brazilian literary canon, a loose application, if you will, of a line of landmark modernist poetry. There is a good deal of play in the words, including musical self-reference and biographical hints.

The bouncy bright up-beat tune is not identified by genre on the album insert, but the track credits indicate that the arrangement was done by the star artist along with a certain Banda do Maracatu Chinfrim (and both of those words, *maracatu* and *chinfrim*, are in the lyric). As is hoped will become evident in the discussion below, the guys may be trying to have a little fun here with cultural exchange. The unidentified ensemble comprises the three Corner Club musicians mentioned in Chapter 3 who play guitar, bass, and percussion here: Nelson Ângelo, Beto Guedes, and Novelli.[1]

---

[1] Luiz Henrique Assis Garcia, "Na esquina do mundo: trocas culturais na música popular brasileira através da obra do Clube da Esquina." PhD thesis. Federal University of Minas Gerais. 2006, p. 232. *Clube da Esquina 2* LP is the location of the song cited in following sentence.

The former and latter had composed (with Milton Nascimento and one other) and then recorded a *samba-enredo* (theme song) for a small samba school in the interior of Brazil with the title "Reis e rainhas do maracatu" (Kings and queens of the maracatu). The Afro-Brazilian folk genre *maracatu* is a mainstay of the carnival season in the city of Recife, where organized groups are called *nações* (nations). A different (rural) kind of *maracatu* exists inland in the state of Pernambuco. The word *maracatu* indicates the procession itself and the percussion-heavy music that accompanies the enactment of an ancient embassy.[2] The music on Chico's cut does not exactly emulate sonically the popular-culture folk referent. At first blush, one does not feel transported to the most typical sounds of the *carnaval* of Recife. But at bottom the *maracatu* speaks, as ethnomusicologist Larry Crook explains:

> The entire song features a repeated two measure groove based on what had, by that time, become codified as a major rhythmic index of the *maracatu*: the syncopated *gonguê* bell pattern used by many traditional maracatu *nações*. On the recording, bass notes articulate the lower part and chords the upper. This is done systematically throughout the song with a few complementary rhythms layered on top of this core groove. … the fade out at the end of the song [is] where this core rhythm is stated in its most basic, unadorned form.[3]

Chico further revealed that this arrangement and the composition itself were forged in the studio. He got the full

---

[2] There are two good print sources in USAmerican ethnomusicology. See Crook, *Brazilian Music*, esp. 157–66; and Murphy, *Music in Brazil*, esp. pp. 86–94.
[3] Professor Larry Crook, personal communication, March 16, 2021.

writing credit, but any of the others may have helped with more than the instrumentation and distribution of parts.

As for the word *chinfrim*, its double meaning is pertinent to both words and music. As a noun, the more contemporary meaning is like a noisy racket, which would be ironic, but a much older meaning is hoedown, street party, popular dance, or even the music for the festivities. As an adjective, *chinfrim* means insignificant, of little value, petty, not much to speak of, also with a silly self-deprecating sense in this context.

Chico's lyric is quite diverting. His stanzas follow the rhyme scheme ABABCB; B and C are the same syllables in all six strophes, only the A lines vary. The B rhyme (-*im*) is the echoing key as it remits to the recurring last three words (*até o fim*), which are the title and the ultimate point: not giving up. What is sung is a self-portrait of a misfit who has had trouble since he was born but keeps on going. There are details to consider strophe to strophe but the initial two lines are the most notable as there is a clear citation of the opening of "Poema de sete faces" ("Poem of Seven Faces") by Brazil's premier Modernist poet Carlos Drummond de Andrade: "Quando nasci veio um anjo torto … " (When I was born, there came a crooked angel).[4] The sung intertextual nod goes "Quando nasci veio um anjo safado" (When I was born there came a rascal of an angel), adding the word *torto* four lines later. Unlike the model, the

---

[4] For a condensed analysis of the poem, see Perrone, *Seven Faces* pp. 13–17; the book also has a sub-chapter on Chico Buarque in the context of national poetry. For a useful comparison of all the many translation of the poem, see Anne Connor, "Poema de Sete+Traduções: A Study of Carlos Drummond de Andrade's 'Poema de Sete Faces.'" *Delos: A Journal of Translation and World Literature*, vol. 32 (2017), pp. 40–59. Open access: http://journals.upress.ufl.edu/delos/article/view/533.

song—which has six sextains and not seven free-verse stanzas of varying length—repeats the angel motif at the end, a circular move more attuned to popular music than literature, yet an affirmation of the poetic homage. In the poem, the subject is instructed to be *gauche* in life, while Chico's character is said to be predestined to go all wrong and bad.

In the second round, the sung persona recalls being a school dropout and the cancellation of his report card. The word for this is *boletim*, which also means bulletin, so there is a hint of press censorship and a link to another rhyme strophes later. Another line says he cannot endure bugles, which can be a sign of aversion to military regimentation. In the next strophe, he has become a singer, very popular in the town Quixeramobim, in the Brazilian state of Ceará, and he professes ignorance of the origin of the form *maracatu*, which is normally associated with the neighboring state of Pernambuco. However, the persistent ethnomusicologist will discover that there actually is a variant of the procession in Fortaleza, Ceará. In stanza four, some "parallel issues" lead to them breaking the singer's instrument, *bandolim*, which further insinuates censorship. Here the word *mazelas* (complaints) could be personal and/or socio-political, but there is an auto-reference to *voz chinfrim*, self-deprecating voicing and rhyming. The penultimate strophe has his wife running off with the owner of the store, from which an insistent ear could even infer American cultural penetration in Brazil. But the tone is inalterably light and the conclusion otherwise:

And, in the end, this song makes evident another point of Chico's aesthetics: humor. This is a trait not often commented upon nor perceived in his work, but it is a fundamental aspect. Whether for the pleasure of language—with wordplay, with interplay of words and melody, with -ins to finalize the various lines, which is accentuated in the singing of the trifling (*chinfrim*) voice—or for the ironic approach, comic or tragicomic.[5]

The apotheosis of appreciation and recognition for any public figure in Rio de Janeiro is to become the subject of the theme song of a leading samba school, an honor reserved for beloved presidents, historical greats, or super artists. Chico Buarque became one of these in 1998 when the theme of the foundational institution G.R.E.S. Estação Primeira de Mangueira was "Chico Buarque da Mangueira."[6] In 1993, he had co-authored with Antônio Carlos Jobim the adroit samba "Piano na Mangueira," which each recorded on his own next album.[7] The typically long text of the tribute *carnaval* samba refers to songs and activities from the whole of Chico's career; two lines specifically allude to "Até o fim"—"Lira de um *anjo* em verso e prosa/De um *querubim* que em verde e rosa" (Lyre of an angel in verse and prose/Of a cherubim who in pink and green [the school's colors]) and one to so many of his song, 1978 or any other year: "Malandro sambista."

<hr />

[5] From the typescript of Ricardo Silvestrin, poet-musician-educator, instructor of the virtual/in-person course Poéticas da MPB.

[6] G R E S stands for *grêmio recreativo escola de samba*, recreational guild samba school. *Estação Primeira* means first station, and *mangueira* is a mango tree, common flora near to where the organization had its meeting place.

[7] For an account of this tune, see https://lyricalbrazil.com/2012/02/28/piano-na-mangueira/. The authors of the 1998 theme samba were Carlinhos das Camisas, Nelson Csipai, Nelson Dalla Rosa, and Vilas Boas. Chico returned the favor later in the year by launching a benefit album for the school.

Até o fim (Buarque)

Quando nasci veio um anjo safado
O chato dum querubim
E decretou que eu tava predestinado
A ser errado assim
Já de saída a minha estrada entortou
Mas vou até o fim
'Inda garoto deixei de ir à escola
Cassaram meu boletim
Não sou ladrão, eu não sou bom de bola
Nem posso ouvir clarim
Um bom futuro é o que jamais me esperou
Mas vou até o fim
Eu bem que tenho ensaiado um progresso
Virei cantor de festim
Mamãe contou que eu faço um bruto sucesso
Em Quixeramobim
Não sei como o maracatu começou
Mas vou até o fim
Por conta de umas questões paralelas
Quebraram meu bandolim
Não querem mais ouvir as minhas mazelas
E a minha voz chinfrim
Criei barriga, a minha mula empacou
Mas vou até o fim
Não tem cigarro acabou minha renda
Deu praga no meu capim
Minha mulher fugiu com o dono da venda
O que será de mim?
Eu já nem lembro pronde mesmo que vou
Mas vou até o fim
Como já disse era um anjo safado

Until the end

When I was born a rascal of an angel,
an annoying cherubim, showed up
and decreed that I was predestined
to be all wrong like this
On departure my road got twisted
But I'm going on until the end
Still a boy I dropped out of school
They cancelled my report card (bulletin)
I'm no crook, I don't play ball well
Nor can I stand to hear bugles
A good future never awaited me
But I'm going on until the end
Yeah, I've been trying to make progress
I became a party singer
Mom said I'm quite a hit
In Quixeramobim [an inland town up north]
I don't know how *maracatu* got started
But I'm going on until the end
Due to some parallel issues
They broke my mandolin
They don't want to hear me moaning
Nor my paltry voice
Got me a paunch, my mule won't budge
But I'm going on until the end
No more smokes, income is gone
My lawn is full of pests
My wife ran off with the shopkeeper
Whatever will become of me?
I don't even remember where I'm going
But I'm going on until the end
As I said it was a rascal of an angel,

O chato dum querubim
Que decretou que eu tava predestinado
A ser todo ruim
Já de saída a minha estrada entortou
Mas vou até o fim

© 1978 Editora Cara Nova; now controlled by Marola Edições Musicais

an annoying cherubim,
who decreed that I was predestined
to be all wrong like this
On departure my highway got twisted
But I'm going on until the end

8 Happy Comrades Abroad

Tracks B4 and B5 of the first *Chico Buarque* illustrate the international side of the multi-genre artist, beyond the Italian connection that goes back to his childhood and brief voluntary exile in 1969-70. One is a watershed cover of a representative instance of Nueva Trova Cubana, the New Song of Cuba, and the other is an update of a shout-out to Portugal in the wake of its own revolution. They are the two shortest items in the album's lineup, but what they lack in temporal extension (or even in musical allure) is overshadowed by the historical content and significance of the recordings.

One cannot gauge the recording of the Cuban song without considering the backstory of its arrival in town. In early 1978, Chico traveled to Europe on business. From Lisbon he caught a flight to Havana as he had accepted an invitation to be a judge for the Casa de las Américas literature prizes, in his case for drama. During his twenty days in Cuba he also met with the imaginative musicians of the collective of the ICAIC (Instituto Cubano del Arte e Industria Cinematográficos), especially the outstanding singer-songwriters Pablo Milanés and Silvio Rodríguez. In February, Chico and three well-known writers returned to Brazil via the international airports of Rio de Janeiro and São Paulo. All were detained by federal police because travel to Cuba was made problematic by the fact that

Figure 6 Chico Buarque, Silvio Rodríguez et al. in Cuba *c.* 1981.
Photo authorized by Marola Edições Musicais and Instituto Antônio
Carlos Jobim.

Figure 7 Chico Buarque, Silvio Rodríguez et al. in Cuba *c.* 1981.
Photo authorized by Marola Edições Musicais and Instituto Antônio
Carlos Jobim.

authoritarian Brazil did not maintain diplomatic relations with
the communist island nation. Chico and wife were taken to a
room and forced to give statements without a lawyer present

since it was a "national security area." All their baggage was seized and searched; books and records were confiscated. This episode of detention was even mentioned at a congressional hearing in Washington DC.

The military agents could not halt the flow of the music, however. Chico soon wrote a version of "Canción por la unidad latinoamericana" (Song for Latin American unity) by Pablo Milanés, which Milton Nascimento and he recorded for the former's 1978 double LP *Clube da Esquina 2*. And Chico would include on his own album of the year "Pequeña serenata diurna" (Small daytime serenade), one of the best short compositions by poet-composer Silvio Rodriguez, who was establishing himself as one of the most brilliant songsmiths in all of Spanish America. Urban ethnomusicology has taken note of the activity: "As a 'strategy of saying', that is, in an attempt to mock the censorship and share with society this sense of non-conformism, musicians and singers of Brazilian Popular Music like Milton Nascimento … and Chico Buarque began to incorporate the songs of … the Cubans Silvio Rodriguez and Pablo Milanés into their playlists and shows."[1] The carioca traveler kept up a keen interest in the many different sounds of the ICAIC and helped fuel a thread of Cuban song in the Brazilian market.[2] In 1982, Chico also wrote versions of two

---

[1] Tânia da Costa Garcia, *The Latin American Songbook in the Twentieth Century: From Folklore to Militancy*. Trans. Christopher Mc Gowan (New York: Lexington, 2019), p. 129.

[2] I was at a reception in the studios of Polygram in 1979. Another guest, the publisher of a recently launched music and sound gear magazine, asked me what I would write about if I had the opportunity. My answer was the sounds of the new Cuba. I never heard from him again, but in a subsequent issue, one of the covers stories was "Exclusivo: a nova música de Cuba," a piece about "the songs from Fidel's island that Brazilians were beginning to hear." *SOM TRES* 5 (1979).

Silvio songs: "Imagina só" (Just imagine) and "Supõe" (Suppose) for recording by Nara Leão, a salient singer of the bossa nova years.[3] With the advent of *abertura* and redemocratization, Chico was an informal cultural ambassador, having a part in a gradual process of rapprochement leading up to the renewal of Brazilian-Cuban diplomatic ties in 1986.

Silvio Rodriguez himself is a great admirer of all Chico's endeavors, and has so demonstrated in statements and creative texts:

> Chico Buarque is a great artist of Brazil, Latin America, and the world. For his theatrical pieces, his poetry, his music, his novels and his way of singing, although he is not of the same opinion regarding his talent as an interpreter. For me it is extremely satisfying to know him and to have shared music and ideas with him, both on stage and off. For all this I put Chico among my preferred authors in my song "Quien fuera."[4]

The 1990 song "Quien fuera" cites Lennon-McCartney, the Chilean genius Violeta Parra, and Chico Buarque. Elsewhere Beethoven is added to the list of preferred composers of the Cuban, who also notes that his Brazilian counterpart had joined the team of those who were singing Cuban songs in solidarity against the US blockade and in favor of internationalism.[5]

---

[3] Nara Leão, *Nasci para bailar*, 1982. In the same year was the LP *Chico Buarque en español,* with versions by Daniel Viglietti of Uruguay who had been following Chico's career for years.

[4] Fernandes, *Textos*, p. 59. Original sent from La Habana, 2003. The song title means something like "who it might be."

[5] Victor Casaus and Luis Rogelio Nogueras, eds., *Silvio: que levante la mano la guitarra* (La Habana: Editorial Letras Cubanas, 2002 [Instituto Cubano del Libro, 1984]), pp. 229, 214.

Pequeña serenata diurna (Rodriguez)

Vivo en un país libre
cual solamente
puede ser libre
en esta tierra,
en este instante,
y soy feliz
porque soy gigante.
Amo a una mujer clara
que amo y me ama
sin pedir nada,
o casi nada,
que no es lo mismo
pero es igual.
Y si esto fuera poco,
tengo mis cantos
que, poco a poco,
muelo y rehago
habitando el tiempo,
como le cuadra a un hombre despierto.
Soy feliz,
soy un hombre
feliz, y quiero
que me perdonen
por este día
los muertos
de mi felicidad.

Source: www.zurrondelaprendiz.cult.cu/canciones/
pequena-serenata-diurna
Used by permission of Silvio Rodriguez and Ediciones Ojalá.
Recorded on *Días y Flores*, 1974

Small Daytime Serenade

I live in a free country
As it can only
be free
In this land
at this moment
And I am happy
because I am a giant
I love a clear woman
Whom I love and who loves me
without asking for anything
Or almost nothing
Which is not the same
But is equal to.
And if this were not much
I have my songs
that little by little
I mull over and remake
inhabiting time
As behooves a man awakened
I am happy
I am a happy
man and I want
that you should pardon me
for this day
the deceased
of my happiness

As for the connection with Portugal, the important date is April 25, 1974, when progressive forces within the military managed to overthrow the authoritarian (fascistically oriented) regime that since 1926 had held a grip on that country and, at increasingly grim costs, its remaining colonies in Africa. The coup-d'état and subsequent far-Left governments constituted *A Revolução dos Cravos*, the Carnation Revolution. This change in the state of affairs did not please the right-wing regime in Brazil, but it did allow Chico Buarque to perform in Portugal freely without fear of persecution there. He composed a circumstantial song called "Tanto mar" (So much sea) in 1975 to pay homage to the achievement of the young officers and their civilian allies, but, to no one's surprise, Brazilian censors banned it for its communist sympathies. In 1978, with political opening on the horizon in Brazil but the Portuguese "revolution" becoming ever more mainstream European, Chico penned an updated version approved for recording.[6] The title was "Tanto mar—2ª edição revista" (So much sea, second revised edition). The musical setting is not clearly Lusitanian, as had been Buarque's aching "Fado tropical" in the *Calabar* drama, which was supposed to sound like the archetypical song form (even though it did not take shape until the nineteenth century and the play is set in the 1630s). The 1978 effort is more like a stage tune (with a dose of folk hand-clapping) with a slow recitative and then a full-band flourish. The first and fifth lines are in past tense to indicate the show was over—the party was nice, pal, your party has wilted—but the third and sixth lines

---

[6] Translations of both original and update, and historical explanation, can be seen at https://lyricalbrazil.com/2012/04/25/tanto-mar/.

express hope: I still keep an old carnation, and they must have left a seed behind. There is an exhortation to sing the Spring (when the Revolution took place) for the singer is needy here (in Brazil still under repressive military rule), hoping for a new whiff of rosemary. If the first version involved sentiments of exile, a younger observer feels, the remake brings metaphors anticipating the return of exiles.[7] In that way, "Tanto mar" is, like "Feijoada completa," quite situated in its time and place, Brazil late nineteen seventies on the verge of a political opening that was calling, full of hope, for song, dance, and nutrition.

---

[7] Sanches, *Tropicalismo*, p. 228.

Tanto mar (Buarque) 1975

Sei que estás em festa, pá

Fico contente

E enquanto estou ausente

Guarda um cravo para mim

Eu queria estar na festa, pá

Com a tua gente

E colher pessoalmente

Uma flor do teu jardim

Sei que há léguas a nos separar

Tanto mar, tanto mar

Sei também quanto é preciso, pá

Navegar, navegar

Lá faz primavera, pá

Cá estou doente

Manda urgentemente

Algum cheirinho de alecrim

© 1975 Editora Musical Cara Nova, now controlled by Marola Edições Musicais

So much sea 1975

Hey pal, I know you're in a party mood
Nice to know that
And since I can't be there for now
Please save me a carnation
I'd like to join the festivities, pal
Along with your people
And pick in person a flower
From your garden
I know we're separated by leagues
So much sea, so much sea
I also know how much, pal,
One must navigate and sail
Where you are, pal, it's Spring!
Over here, I'm plain sick
Urgent! send some fragrance
Of rosemary

Tanto mar, 2ª edição, 1978

Foi bonita a festa, pá
Fiquei contente
E inda guardo, renitente
Um velho cravo para mim
Já murcharam tua festa, pá
Mas certamente
Esqueceram uma semente
Nalgum canto do jardim
Sei que há léguas a nos separar
Tanto mar, tanto mar
Sei também quanto é preciso, pá
Navegar, navegar
Canta a primavera, pá
Cá estou carente
Manda novamente
Algum cheirinho de alecrim

So much sea, second edition

The party was lovely, pal
It was so nice to know
And I insist on keeping
an aged carnation for myself
They've made your party wilt, pal
But they must have
forgotten a seed
in some corner of the garden
I know we're separated by leagues
So much sea, so much sea
I know too, pal, how one must
Navigate, must sail
Sing the praises of Spring, pal
Here I'm still needy
Send again fragrance
of rosemary

9 A Cup, a Chalice, a Gem

The most authoritative source on the history of Brazilian song begins each year-by-year entry with the overall *destaques* (highlights, features, standouts). For 1978, the second work considered is "Cálice" (Gilberto Gil-Chico Buarque).[1] While this was indeed the discographic birth of the celebrated composition, it was composed in 1973, and there is a multifaceted and rather revealing backstory to tell. After the first *Chico Buarque*, "Cálice" continued to make its presence felt as an attention-grabbing instance of musical history; it is no stretch to say that this one of the most outstanding and consequential songs of the entire MPB repertory.

"Cálice" is a slow, brooding protest song with a punch-packing lyric, powered by an idiosyncratic homophone. Here, a close listening to the arrangement follows a consideration of the text.[2] While both words and music are co-written, the title

[1] Jairo Severiano and Zuza Homem de Mello, *A canção no tempo: 85 anos de músicas brasileiras. Vol. 2 1958–1985* (São Paulo: editor 34, 1998), p. 241. Since Gil was on his way from the Polygram label to the new-kid-in-town competitor WEA, there was some sort of booking glitch and Milton was hired to record his parts. Even better for continuity with the 1976 disc and the even greater voice.

[2] With respect to translations, there is a "literary" rendering in Perrone, *Masters*, p. 33 ff. There are numerous amateur (nonnative) translations on websites dedicated to song texts, e.g. lyrictranslated.com, or worldwide music, e.g. musicmatch.com; in the present case the most useful post, since it comes with

Figure 8 Chico Buarque and Gilberto Gil *c.* 1980; photo by and courtesy of Elena Carminati, authorized by her and Gegê Edições.

and keyword are Gil's, the extrapolations are Chico's. The former wrote stanzas one and three (sung by Milton Nascimento on the 1978 LP), while the latter added two and four. All together the strophes configure a subject driven to distraction and despair, silenced by an (implied) authority with oppressive designs. The refrain, intoned before each stanza, is modeled on biblical passages: "Father, take away (remove) this cup from me" (Mark 14:36, Matthew 26:39, Luke 22:42). This evocation of the prelude to the Passion, Christ's betrayal, and the crucifixion all suggest suffering and persecution. Here, too, the semanteme of drink/drinking is set, in advance of significant references to

---

a link to a videoclip with press photos of street repression and explanations line by line, is https://www.reddit.com/r/Music/Comments/1siijd/song_analysis_chico_buarque. See also the textual commentary in https://www.wordsinthebucket.com/calice-chico-buarque-gilberto-gil.

liquid and inebriation throughout (*de vinho tinto de sangue*/ with wine red with blood). The fulcrum is the word *cálice* (cup, chalice), which is pronounced exactly the same as *cale-se* (shut up!), an imperative with a clear connection to censorship, imposed silence, gag orders, and victimization.

Each eight-line stanza has ponderous images. The first mentions a bitter beverage, pain, a shuttered mouth, dead reality, lies, brute force. The second includes nocturnal self-damnation, inhumane screams, silence, senselessness, a monster. The third (and most mysterious to most ears) fat pigs, used knives, imprisoned words, drunken sprees. The fourth concludes with self-poisoning, losing one's head and judgment, inebriated oblivion. The macabre penultimate line "I want to sniff diesel fumes" refers in general to an actual practice of torture by security forces, and specifically to the death of one Stuart Angel, whose mouth was strapped to a car's exhaust pipe during a torture session. As the song progresses, with allusions to corresponding parts of the body, the facilities of speech, feeling, and reason are "tortured" and "shut up." Once the subject refers to "losing his head," self-destructive delusions have set in and dismemberment has occurred. So, one can clearly comprehend that the attractiveness of the lyric is in its suggestive imagery not in depiction of pretty things. It is easy to agree that all the images in this "protest song" can be interpreted in terms of people oppressed by a nasty regime.[3]

---

[3] Aleilton Fonseca, "Cálice que não se cala." In Fernandes, *Poeta*, p. 36.

An Italian critic, whose insights have been lauded by José Miguel Wisnik, observed in the early 1980s that this is

> one of the most beautiful compositions by the carioca if not the absolutely most beautiful. First for its vibrant force, full of emotion, hardly contained in the superb recording together with Milton Nascimento, and then for the decisive arrangement, so sober and essential, leaving the voices the task of sustaining the piece for much of its duration.[4]

Half of the writing credit, of course, must go to Gilberto Gil, and half the beauty perceived resides in the recording not the composition per se. And the vocal sustenance is the first half of the performance. But the perception of core beauty is wholly spot on. Arrangement includes both how things are sung and the distribution of instruments with their attack. Choral vocables (ooh-ooh-ooh-ooh) precede the song proper, simulating a liturgy. The pivotal homophone will become more prominent to draw attention to its double-edged intent. One analyst even believes that the refrain is "an aggregating appeal of conscience" and that the song is "an act of sacrificial exorcism of the regime … it has an operatic quality to the degree that it contains a narrative, cyphered in the musical score and in the double-meaning semantics of the lyric."[5] The most detailed study of the song proposes that the melodic shape of the refrain intensifies the sense of suffering, and

[4] Paolo Scarnecchia, *Musica popolare brasiliana* (Milano: Gammalibri, 1983), pp. 29–30.

[5] Fonseca, p. 36.

Cálice (Gil-Buarque)

Pai, afasta de mim esse cálice
Pai, afasta de mim esse cálice
Pai, afasta de mim esse cálice
De vinho tinto de sangue
Como beber dessa bebida amarga
Tragar a dor, engolir a labuta
Mesmo calada a boca, resta o peito
Silêncio na cidade não se escuta
De que me vale ser filho da santa
Melhor seria ser filho da outra
Outra realidade menos morta
Tanta mentira, tanta força bruta
Como é difícil acordar calado
Se na calada da noite eu me dano
Quero lançar um grito desumano
Que é uma maneira de ser escutado
Esse silêncio todo me atordoa
Atordoado eu permaneço atento
Na arquibancada pra a qualquer momento
Ver emergir o monstro da lagoa
De muito gorda a porca já não anda
De muito usada a faca já não corta
Como é difícil, pai, abrir a porta
Essa palavra presa na garganta
Esse pileque homérico no mundo
De que adianta ter boa vontade
Mesmo calado o peito, resta a cuca
Dos bêbados do centro da cidade
Talvez o mundo não seja pequeno
Nem seja a vida um fato consumado
Quero inventar o meu próprio pecado

Cup/Chalice

Father, take away this cup from me
Father, take away this cup from me
Father, take away this cup from me
This cup of wine red with blood
How to partake of this bitter drink
Swallow the pain, gulp our daily toil
Though my mouth is sealed, my breast remains
No one hears the silence in the city
What good is it to be a son of a saint
It would be better to be a son of a …
Another less lifeless reality
So many lies, so much brute force
How hard it is to awaken silenced
If I am damned in the still of the silent night
I want to unleash an inhuman scream
Which is a way to be heard
All this silence makes me senseless
Senseless yet still watchful
For the lake-monster to emerge
In the grandstand at any moment
The sow is so fat she can't move anymore
The knife is so used it can't cut anymore
It is so difficult, father, to open the door
These words caught in my throat
This Homeric spree in the world
What good will good will do
Though my heart is sealed, there are still
The heads of the drunks downtown
Perhaps the world is not so small
Nor life a consummated fact
I want to invent my own sins

Quero morrer do meu próprio veneno
Quero perder de vez tua cabeça
Minha cabeça perder teu juízo
Quero cheirar fumaça de óleo diesel
Me embriagar até que alguém me esqueça

© 1973 Marola Edições Musicais, Gegê Produções.

that syllabic accents and variations condense the historical experience of revolt and criticism.[6] In the first two sections, the singing voice is foregrounded, which, together with light acoustic-guitar arpeggios, creates a subdued doleful mood. In the third and fourth sections, a loud addition becomes effective: pounding drums and a strident electric-guitar figure enter aggressively while the vocal presentation is more forceful. These sonorous modifications are reinforcement for the establishment of mood in the words. The backup singers practically shout the words *pai* (Father) and *cálice/cale-se* (cup/shut up) with insistence, from the third stanza until the end. This choral counterpoint is carried out in a stern, authoritative tone, echoing the exchange between victim and oppressor implied in the lyric. The concluding four lines are sung a cappella, as if engulfed in a surrounding silence. As the instruments have dropped out, there is a sense of isolation, abandonment, defeat. The end is abrupt to finish off this effect.

---

[6] Walter Garcia, "Notas sobre 'Cálice' (2010, 1973, 1978, 2011)." *Música popular em revista*, vol. 2, no. 2 (2014), pp. 22 and 27. His paper considers the 2010 and 2011 off-shoots of the song seen below.

I want to die by my own poison
I want to lose once and for all your head
My head to lose your judgement
I want to sniff diesel fumes
Get intoxicated until someone forgets me.

Most of the preceding observations about arrangement do not apply to the original attempted performance of "Cálice" because it was just two guys and their acoustic guitars. The genesis and aftermath of the stage baptism are pregnant with tones, moans, and overtones. Sensing the end of the era of competitive song festivals in 1973, the Polydor label, whose stable was the most populated and luxurious in the Brazilian music industry, decided instead to have a "festival" to showcase the considerable talent of their cast. A four-day show was planned in which each star artist would sing one hit, one new song, and one song done in collaboration with a colleague. Chico was paired with Gilberto Gil, who began to write a tune for them the day after Good Friday.[7] He took the foundational idea of the refrain and a first verse over to Chico's house. He grasped the opportunity of the homophone and they worked on the music. Gil wrote another stanza, Chico his own pair, and they finalized melody and harmony in a second meeting. The label quickly submitted the song to the bureau of state

[7] The main source for this story is Gilberto Gil, *Todas as letras* (São Paulo: Companhia das Letras, 1996), p. 139.

control, which did not approve.[8] Nevertheless, in an act of "civil disobedience" Gil and Chico tried to sing a disfigured version of the song on stage at the convention center in São Paulo (Phono 73, Palácio de Convenções do Anhembi, May 11–13, 1973). For some three and a half minutes, they hummed the melody, some grammelot (vocables, ad hoc gibberish, nonsense words, random phrases, like menu excerpts) and even snippets of the lyric. Once some of the actual words, including "cálice," were heard things got ugly. Chico's house microphone was turned off, and when alternate mics were tried, they too were cut off, a turn that literally embodied the *cale-se* meaning of the refrain. Everyone assumed government authorities had intervened.

It has taken years and decades to sort through the evidence to determine what really went on that night. There are eye-witness and participant accounts, hearsay, label outlooks, sound recordings, television and film footage (the label was planning to do a movie release), coverage in the popular and mainstream press, music criticism, editorial pieces, academic notices, and more recently blogs and virtual discussion groups. It was rumored and reported that police had come on stage to stop the song since it had been proscribed, agents removing

---

[8] Phonogram reported that the text of "Cálice" was sent to their office on May 3, and then taken to the Censorship Service in Rio, which did not liberate it. Next they sent a letter to the São Paulo branch trying to get an authorization for a one-time performance at the festival, which was also denied (*Folha de São Paulo*, May 18, 1973). Curiously, the lyric was not banned from print. It was published in the column "Música popular" by Julio Hungria in the *Jornal do Brasil* (Sunday May 13, 1973) and in *Jornal da tarde* (May 12, 1973) and a week later in *A ponte*, a bulletin board at the School of Arts and Communication at USP, where Gil would sing the song live.

one microphone after another. That proved to be false, as the house sound was brought down in the control booth not via any unplugging on stage. The incident was captured on film and broadcast on television (Bandeirantes Network) on Christmas Day, 1978, during the early stages of liberalization and redemocratization, but the men seen grabbing mic stands are not law enforcement but stage hands and even members of the group MPB4 who were trying to help by switching muffled mics for live ones. In any case, there is little doubt that officials played the decisive role. Moby, preoccupied with the "climate" of those times, notes that even the establishment rag *Veja* reported that there were long-haired underground cops at the show mingling with artists.[9] More to the point, federal censors were in the control booth "encouraging" the sound technicians to perform the task of silencing the offending singers. For the sake of history and reconstruction, the good news is that while the house sound was turned off, the microphones were still getting signals to the recording equipment. So there are ways to hear quite a bit of what Gil and Chico tried to sing and say.

Chico's most quoted words in the minutes following the banishment are "Censors, sons of bitches!" and "They are really rubbing me the wrong way. This business of turning off the sound was not in the program! Sure, it was in the program that I could not sing this song or 'Ana de Amsterdam' [censored

[9] Alberto Moby, *Sinal Fechado: a música popular brasileira sob censura* (Rio de Janeiro: Obra Aberta, 1994), pp. 134–5. This under-recognized study compares censorship during the Estado Novo 1937–45 and the military regime 1964–85. The best commentary plus video is at https://soulart.org/artes/musica/phono-73-o-canto-de-um-povo 5 minutes of Chico with no other interspersed footage. See also www.youtube.com/watch?v=oXGDM.

song from *Calabar*]. I won't sing either of the two. But turning off the sound, that was uncalled for." He was upset with Phonogram for turning off the mics and threatened to leave the label. But the president of operations stated that they were on his side against the censors, who thought that are all the musicians were "commies," and that the fault was therefore all theirs.[10]

After the festival "Cálice" was still banned but it did circulate, like other censored songs, among friends and at a few restricted venues, most notably in a full performance by Gil at a show at the University of São Paulo, where he was asked to sing the song over and over.[11] The proscribed status lasted until the recordings by Buarque and others, with which it became a top-ten airplay song in late 1978 and early 1979, busting records for airplay. Between December 1978 and February 1979 there were 1,500 executions (plays) on AM radio and TV.[12] The media history of the composition and the incident continue with the above-cited Christmas TV broadcast in 1978, and nonstop print mentions. In 1997, *Phono 73—O canto de um povo* (The singing of a people) which had been a series of LPs in the early seventies, was released as a three-CD set, with tunes by Chico and Gil other than "Cálice." The very release was an excuse to relive the stage trouble in 1973. As Sean Stroud (p. 69) has

[10] Luiz Fernando Vianna, "Phono 73 registra história da MPB." *Folha de São Paulo* November 15, 2005.
[11] Priscila Gomes Correa, "Performance e resistência no Festival Phono 73." Annals of *XXIX Simpósio de história nacional: contra os preconceitos: história de democracia.* p. 6. https://www.snh2017.anpuh.org/site/anais. For her, Gil's song with Chico was far and away the most important moment of the festival.
[12] Sheyla Castro Diniz, "Denúncia política e contracultura: o show 'proibido' de Gilberto Gil na Poli / USP (1973)." *Teoria e cultura* vol. 13, no. 2 (2018), p. 170.

noted, a turning point in the critical reception was the release of a set in 2005 with two CDs and a DVD, which included footage of the fateful incident. Because of deterioration of the film originals, the DVD pressing is only 35 minutes long (of 4 nights of shows with multiple acts) with technical problems and uneven sound quality, but there is enough to work with. The sound and images that survived "can illuminate up to a decade of Brazilian history, for they show traditions, inventions and rebellions, a potential synthesis for the understanding of the complex relationships among an authoritarian state, an expanding market and one of the most popular arts of Brazilian society, music" (Gomes Correa, p. 1).

That historical value is seen anew in three enactments. In 2010, rapper Criolo Doido (Crazy Creole) recorded a performance of a parody (parallel ode)-pastiche-homage to "Cálice" which he posted to YouTube, to considerable acclaim, affirming the legacy of the song, and the voices of Milton Nascimento and Chico Buarque. It is a moment when rap legitimizes MPB as raw material for peripheral culture too.[13] For his part Chico recognized the post, and in his show-tour of 2011 he responded with "Rap de Cálice" in which he states that he and Gil have been welcomed to the club: "Um dia eu vi uma parada assim no YouTube/E disse 'que os pariu, parece o Cálice/Aquela cantiga minha e do Gil" (One day I saw this cool deal on YouTube/And I said son of a…, it's like Cálice/ That canticle of mine with Gil).[14] From new popular culture to

---

[13] Walter Garcia, "Notas," p. 111. With these follow-up segments, this is even more so the most complete study of the song and its situations.

[14] There is a commercial DVD of this show-tour. Garcia transcribes most of the text.

political problems, Chico and Gil could be counted on. In 2018, they did a duet of their famous song at Festival Lula Livre, an outside venue in Rio de Janeiro to protest the unjust arrest of former president Luiz Inácio da Silva on trumped-up charges

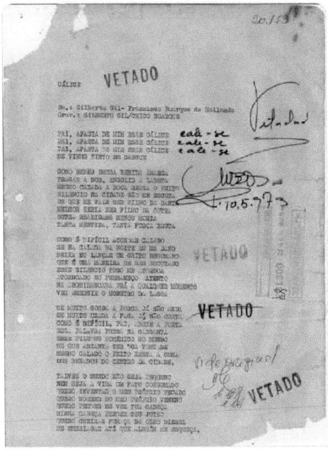

Figure 9 Typescript of lyric of "Cálice" stamped by federal censors (1973); public domain.

(his "conviction" has since been overturned by higher courts). Historical echoes marked the presentation and moved the crowd, estimated to be 50,000. In a curious twist, Chico began to sing with his mic turned off. He later sang "As caravanas" (Caravans, 2017), a song that bemoans racist middle-and upper-class attitudes toward poor young blacks and "Deus lhe pague" (May God reward you), one of his magnificent protest songs from the *Construção* days. These reprises established the coherent reunion of Chico and Gil.[15] In other shows, Gil, who had avoided recording the song himself, sang it with Milton Nascimento. Only one song in Mr. Buarque's career can rival "Cálice," with its definitive recording in 1978, for lasting historical significance, and that is the subject of the next chapter.

---

[15] Leonardo Lichote, "Chico e Gil voltam a cantar 'Cálice' juntos após 45 anos.'" *O globo.* July 29, 2018.

10 In Spite of You, Tomorrow Will Be Another Day

The most authoritative source on the history of Brazilian song begins each year-by-year chapter with the overall *destaques* (highlights, features, standouts). For 1970 the number-one work is Chico's "Apesar de você" (In spite of you) which was released as a 45 RPM single.[1] This feel-good avenging samba, composed as repression was intensifying in the wake of the "official" decree of dictatorship, has had quite an active history, fifty years and counting. The definitive recording was as the last track on a 33 1/3 LP, the first *Chico Buarque*, but the backstory was legend by the time the 1978 album was pressed.

In early 1970, as Chico was returning from a "voluntary exile" in Italy (where he had recorded two LPs) he got some advice from bossa nova giant and family friend Vinícius de Moraes: "Come back making a lot of noise." It was a couple of months ahead of Brazil's opportunity to win their unprecedented third world cup of soccer, and the country was experiencing a patriotic campaign of boosterism. While so-called previous

---

[1] Severiano and Homem de Mello, *A cancao no tempo*, p. 151. The flip side of the 45 was a tune with Vinicius de Moraes, "Desalento" (Being down).

censorship (having to submit for approval before recording) was in place to prevent songs with words unfavorable to the military regime, radio stations were playing rah-rah songs like "Pra frente Brasil" (Onward Brazil!) and "Eu te amo, meu Brasil" (I love you my Brazil). Chico replied, making noise, with a "true protest song." "Apesar de você" was addressed to an unnamed "you," bemoaning loss of liberty and imagining nicer times, "in spite of you, tomorrow will be another day" per the refrain. Chico asked canonical Modernist poet Manuel Bandeira if his song would be caught by the filter of censorship. The reply was "only if they see *segundas intenções* (ulterior motives)."[2] And what happened is an oft-told tale.

Nelson Motta has been a music critic since the 1960s. His latest book is *101 canções que tocaram o Brasil* (101 songs that touched/played Brazil), which naturally includes more than one by Chico Buarque, the most political being "Apesar de você." Once composed the song was presented to staff at Phonogram, who sent the text to the Federal Department of Censorship, not expecting approval. But the censor in charge let it pass, so it was recorded immediately. It was a massive hit, eventually reaching 100,000 copies sold (a gold record, and radio favorite). No one could believe it: "an extroverted samba, cheerful and dissolute, singing what so many people wanted to hear and say, a direct message to the dictatorship, abusing and bruising. A great samba that cleansed our souls. People sang it immediately as a hymn of resistance, a challenge and hope." In early 1971, the *Jornal do Brasil* published an article suspecting that the targeted "you" in the harangue of song

---

[2] Homem, *Histórias de canções*, p. 58.

might be the military president of the land, which touched off a fierce reaction. Soon the tune was banned (on May 7), from radio and sales, all store copies were confiscated, the army invaded the factory to seize and burn discs. It was, however, too late: the record had been available for five months and there were lots of extant 45s in homes, plus tape copies, and folks already knew how to sing it.[3] The guilty lax censor was punished, but little more could be done. Most importantly, and luckily, they did not think to destroy the master tape of the recording, which made another edition possible.[4] Between 1970 and 1978, and the relaxation of censorship, the song, or key parts such as the refrain, continued to circulate in opposition circles, which were considerable.

"Apesar de você" is a prime example of the samba-duplex, in which the tricky malandro composer writes something that seems to be one thing but can totally be another, as in a brash social statement masquerading as an amatory complaint. To no one's surprise, Chico was summoned to testify regarding his big hit. Military interrogators asked him who is "you" in this song, and he had two plausible replies. He told them it was a "mulher muito mandona e autoritária" (a very bossy authoritarian bitch), which taken literally would be in the tradition of macho-lament songs, but metaphorically could signify a terrible maternal state, i.e. the regime. Chico also took one image from the lyric and argued that he had written the

---

[3] Nelson Motta, *101 canções que tocaram o Brasil* (Rio de Janeiro: Estação Brasil, 2016), p. 105.
[4] The wording in Severiano and Homem de Mello implies that in 1978 the original was re-mastered. Chico himself said he used the "original arrangement" so younger kids could hear what had gone down in 1970.

song about a rooster that somehow believed that day only broke due to his song (an allusion to the organizing conceit of the celebrated film *Orfeu negro/Black Orpheus*, 1959), until one dawn when the rooster caught on that day broke "in spite of him." Samba-MPB singer Clara Nunes actually recorded a cover believing it was "a lyric about a lovers' spat and quarrel." As "punishment" she was forced to sing for the armed forces' own "olympics" in 1971. Chico was not arrested for all this, but he did become Public Enemy #1 for the blue meanies of the censorship division, who would not let him alone for the next seven years. Chico later revealed that his "you" was not specifically the military president, but the entire regime, everything, the context, the system of power as a whole.[5]

As early as 1972, this samba of impact was fulfilling extra-musical, even international, roles. A human-rights group in the United States (CARIB, Committee Against Repression in Brazil) made an educational slide show about torture and the grim situation in Brazil to show to concerned parties, especially in advance of a scheduled visit by the Brazilian president. The heated song was used to close the presentation, with an explanation of the chorus and the process of censorship.[6]

---

[5] Regina Zappa, *Chico Buarque para todos*. 5th edition (Rio de Janeiro: Relume Dumará Prefeitura do Rio de Janeiro, 2000), qtd. by Fernandes, *Textos*, p. 32. Despite all they admired him: in 2020–21 a cartoon on social media has a citizen asking "Was there anything good about the Dictatorship?" A military general replies: "Chico Buarque's songs!" Even his enemies liked him and his work!

[6] James N. Green, *We Cannot Remain Silent: Opposition to the Brazilian Military Dictatorship in the United States* (Durham, NC: Duke University Press, 2010), p. 273. The 2009 translation of this book has the quite indicative title *Apesar de vocês*, suggested by the author himself, which is pluralized to indicate Brazilian leaders and American connivance.

Back in Brazil, one of the most widely circulated photos in the history of national journalism shows a crowd on a São Paulo street at a massive pre-congressional election rally of the opposition PMDB (Democratic Brazilian Movement Party) in 1974; the banner under which they march reads "Amanhã vai ser outro dia," which is the initial refrain of "Apesar de você."[7] A salient public utilization of the musical reference but very far from the last.

As seen in the course of this account of the first *Chico Buarque*, his previous content album, *Meus caros amigos*, has several notable connections with the album that solidified "Apesar de você." The always reliable historian Napolitano observes in wide perspective:

> For Chico Buarque politics emerges as an existential condition and permeates all spheres of private and public life, synthesizing an experience of time that oscillates between critical melancholy and ironic euphoria. In the two albums that synthesize the music of the political opening in Chico Buarque—*Meus caros amigos* (1976) and *Chico Buarque* (1978)—the songs seem to oscillate between these two expressive poles. From the first we have "Corrente," "Meu caro amigo," "O que será (A flor da terra)." From the second, "Cálice." "Homenagem ao malandro" and "Apesar de você."[8]

The samba "Corrente" (Chain/Current) is an ingenious samba of resistance whose words can be heard (or read on

---

7 December 12, 1979 in the mainstream news magazine *Veja*. Currently on countless internet sites.

[8] Napolitano Marcos, "Brazilian Popular Music: The Soundtrack of the Political Opening (1975/1982)," *Estudos avançados*, vol. 24, no. 69 (2010), p. 392.

the lyric sheet) forward and backward, with different results of course. An apparent *mea culpa* for the "sin" of "Apesar de você" in 1970, it is actually another two-edged sword swung at the less-than-liked authorities.[9] When he recorded "Corrente," Chico could not have known that the veil of censorship would be lifting before too long, so the continuity with the remake of "Apesar de você" would end up being even more satisfying.

After ten other tracks on the 1978 LP, the 1970 samba commences the final advance of the album in style. A chorus (MPB4) is faded in singing three times "Amanhã vai ser outro dia" (tomorrow will be another day). The body of the song text will comprise six sections (65 short utterances in 5 1/2 verses of 12 rhyme-schemed lines). After the initial verse (V1) each of the subsequent ones is introduced by the refrain "Apesar de você amanhã há de ser outro dia" (tomorrow is [bound] to be another day), in an archaic future form, which can also suggest obligation or probability. At first, there is just lead voice and limited accompaniment (guitar, bass, hand percussion), but typical instruments are added as the samba grows. By V2, the vocal lead is doubled, and by V3 it is a veritable chorus, a public affair, and the backing vocals continue doubling the melody with vocables until the end. V5 is just five lines of words until the concluding "etc. et al" (etc. and such and such) until a cascade of vocables (la-la-la) fading until a final barely audible refrain.

Although there is a mention of poetry, the discourse here is scarcely poetic, rather the language is conversational, like a

---

9 See, in English, Perrone, *Masters*, pp. 35–7, and, in a newer take in Portuguese, "A força dos elos da 'Corrente.'" In Fernandes, *Poeta*, pp. 91–8.

spurned lover talking to his ex- and vowing payback in second person.[10] Throughout, the structure of the text banks on a "free play of antitheses" in succession, interspersed with the refrain: "today vs. tomorrow." All that is repressed vs. all that will surge anew.[11] In V1 he acknowledges that "you" are in charge and that his people are downcast and turning the other way to speak. References to "this state," "darkness," and "sin" could be just the inter-personal situation, but can easily be taken to mean the unwanted government. V2 asks where "you" will hide from euphoric change and how "you" will prohibit a cock from crowing and new waters of love, which can also be metaphorical. V3 is the most vindictive strophe, vowing to charge extra interest for damages done, also conceivably tied to the "economic miracle" that shook Brazil in the 1970s. There is another request to "dis-invent" sadness. V4 brings a new day, a new garden, and gratifying laughter. V5 sings of rebirth, poetry, a sky clearing, and singing in your face. In each strophe, it is possible to imagine the words being directed to a former partner who deserves punition, but associations with a nasty authority are easy to make.

The precise way that "Apesar de você" is composed and sung can be heard to fortify the message of resistance. It exemplifies that "juncture of linguistic articulation and somatic mobilization that does not merely *convey* the *desire*

---

[10] See translations in Victoria Broadus, lyricalbrazil.com, Claus Schreiner, *Música Brasileira: A History of the Popular Music and the People of Brazil* (London: Marion Boyars, 1993), and the imaginative literary Spiller, www.chicobuarquetranslated.com or short Amazon e-book.

[11] Adélia Bezerra de Meneses, *Desenho mágico: poesia e política em Chico Buarque* (São Paulo: Hucitec, 1982), p. 77.

for emancipation; rather … in a dual downward and upward melodic-discursive movement (…) it rehearses, enacts, and performs its *realization,* rendering actions as words, and words as actions."[12] And years after the discographic register of this deserved scolding, the song continues to be used for public purposes.

There have been various employments of the song in Brazil and abroad, illustrating the social uses of popular music. For instance, in 1985 the Archdiocese of São Paulo published a report on abuses during the military regime: *Brasil nunca mais!* The frontispiece of chapter XI of James N. Green's monograph has a photo of the cover of the English translation, *Torture in Brazil* (1986), and as epigraph cites the refrain of "Apesar de você" with a gloss.[13] In April 2016, the Rio club Fundição Progresso had a packed event in defense of democracy, and the crowd sang "Apesar de você" in ironic homage to conspirators for a coup-d'état. In May of the same year, the prefecture of São Paulo sponsored an exposition "Os Trabalhadores e os 100 anos do Samba" (Workers and 100 years of samba), which included large posters on lamp posts on the miracle mile of Avenida Paulista. In front of the headquarters of corporate society (FIESP is the federation of industries of the state), hung a grand banner with a picture of Chico dressed as malandro with his famous refrain in large print. Before long the image was vandalized with black paint, a sign of right-wing anger. In August, Chico sang his landmark tune at the

[12] David Treece, "Bringing Brazil's Resistance Songs to London: Words and Music in Translation." *Veredas: Revista da Associação Internacional de Lusitanistas* (2018), p. 72. Original emphasis.
[13] Photographic reproduction in Green, *We Cannot Remain Silent*, p. 355.

once-venerable Rio venue Canecão at an event to protest the closing of Ministry of Education and Culture.

One of the most imaginative international homages to Chico and the struggle of the Brazilian people for democracy had happened in June 2016 in Paris when the Orchestre Debout (marching big band) did a public performance of "Apesar de você," which was advertised and discussed on social media; it was also listed by a Brazilian outlet as one of the most viral videos of the year against the temporary president who assumed after a parliamentary coup had ousted the legitimate president Rousseff.[14]

Fast forward to 2020 and boisterous popular protests against the outrages of the Bolsonaro administration. The timid mainstream press may not have focused sufficiently on outcry but social media was abuzz with anti-executive posts and news of demonstrations. One resident educator reported that every evening for three months and counting a neighbor would blast "Apesar de você" on speakers as people banged on pots, pans, and percussion instruments while shouting "genocidal, militia man, bandit, fascist, out!"[15] An act with much more cachet was a multiple-artist-sponsored manifesto against the disastrous neo-fascist presidency. The document was posted bilingually:

Composed fifty years ago by Chico Buarque de Holanda, "Apesar de você" (In spite of you) is an eloquent musical manifesto against the authoritarianism and censorship that

[14] Web coagulator, *Brasil de Fato*, São Paulo, July 19, 2016.
[15] Tania S. Bastos, post on Facebook 6-18-20.

inhibited human liberties and fundamental rights during the Brazilian dictatorship. Today, on International Human Rights Day [December10], we launch an audio-visual manifesto against violations of human rights and in favor of freedom of expression and democracy.[16]

The musical support was a new recording of the hymn by Bahian pop star Daniela Mercury, a cover that, as of this writing, continues to get airplay in Brazil and around the world. Protests against the maniacal president continued in early 2021, with the go-to song invoked anew in neighborhoods of Rio de Janeiro.[17] One other indicator of enduring resonance were quotations of the refrain sewn onto protective facemasks sold online during the Covid-19 pandemic.[18]

More than fifty years out "Apesar de você" remains Brazil's foremost song of resistance and affirmation of hope against forces of evil. While the joyous samba was initially launched in 1970, it was firmly set in sound stone in 1978 on the first *Chico Buarque*, an LP whose historical import continues to be proven year after year.

---

[16] I am grateful to Professor José Augusto Pádua for sending me this (Facebook 12-12-20; #VideoManifestio #ApesardeVoce #DanielaMercury) and other pertinent notices.

[17] For example, "Barulhaço muito bom de novo aqui em Botafogo. Voltamos com 'Apesar de você' nas caixas de som. O genocida tem que cair antes de terminar a carnificina!" #ForaBolsonaro "Luciano Monteiro, Facebook post, 1-21-21 (A really good racket again in our borough here. We brought the song back in our loud speakers. The genocidal man has to fall before completing his slaughter. Bolsonaro Out!")

[18] These were offered on a Facebook Fan Page for Chico Buarque.

Apesar de você (Buarque)

Amanhã vai ser outro dia (3x)
Hoje você é quem manda,
falou, tá falado
Não tem discussão, não
A minha gente hoje anda
Falando de lado
e olhando pro chão, viu?
Você que inventou esse estado
Que inventou de inventar
toda a escuridão
Você que inventou o pecado
Esqueceu-se de inventar
o perdão
Apesar de você
amanhã há de ser
outro dia
Eu pergunto a você
Onde vai se esconder
da enorme euforia?
Como vai proibir
Quando o galo insistir em cantar?
Água nova brotando
E a gente se amando
sem parar
Quando chegar o momento,
esse meu sofrimento
Vou cobrar com juros, juro
Todo esse amor reprimido,
esse grito contido
Este samba no escuro
Você que inventou a tristeza

In Spite of You

Tomorrow is going to be another day (3x)
Today, you're in charge
Said and done, 'nuff said
There's no argument, nope
These days my folks are turning
Aside to speak and
looking down, see?
You who invented this state,
Contrived the invention of
All this darkness
You who invented sin
Forgot to invent
forgiveness
In spite of you
Tomorrow will be
Another day
I ask you
where you will hide
From the enormous euphoria
How will you prohibit it
When the rooster insists on crowing?
New waters bubbling up
And people loving each other
without stopping
When the time comes,
I swear I'm going to charge
For this suffering of mine
with interest I swear
All this love held down
These shouts held back
This samba in the dark
You who invented sadness

Ora, tenha a fineza de desinventar
Você vai pagar e é dobrado
Cada lágrima rolada
nesse meu penar
Apesar de você
amanhã há de ser
outro dia
Inda pago pra ver
o jardim florescer
Qual você não queria
Você vai se amargar
Vendo o dia raiar
sem lhe pedir licença
E eu vou morrer de rir
Que esse dia há de vir
antes do que você pensa
Apesar de você
amanhã há de ser
outro dia
Você vai ter que ver
a manhã renascer
E esbanjar poesia
Como vai se explicar
vendo o céu clarear
De repente, impunemente?
Como vai abafar
Nosso coro a cantar
na sua frente?
Apesar de você
amanhã há de ser
outro dia
Você vai se dar mal,
etcetera e tal

Now kindly un-invent it
You're gonna pay two times over
Every tear that I've shed
In this grief of mine
In spite of you
Tomorrow will be
another day
I'll still pay to see
The garden blooming
As you did not desire
You'll be bitter
Seeing the day break
Without asking your permission
And I'm gonna die laughing
For that day is bound to come
Sooner than you may think
In spite of you
Tomorrow will be
another day
You'll have to see
The morning being reborn
And overflowing poetry
How will you explain yourself
As you see the sky clear up,
suddenly, with impunity?
How are you gonna muffle
Our chorus singing
Right in front of you
In spite of you
Tomorrow is going to be
another day
it's gonna go bad for you
Etcetera and such and such

Laraiá laraiá lá
Laraiá laraiá, laraiá laraiá
Lá laiá lá
Laraiá laraiá, laraiá laraiá
Larararā
Apesar de você …

© 1970 Editora Musical Cara Nova, now controlled by Marola Edições Musicais

Figure 10 Sheet music cover "Apesar de você" (1970); Cara Nova/ Arlequim music publisher, São Paulo, Brazil; courtesy of Waldemar Jorge Menendez Marchetti.

La la-la, la la-la
La la-la, la la-la
La la-la, la la-la
La la-la, la la-la
La la-la, la la-la
In spite of you

11 Outro: Rio, Brazil, the World

From the star artist's soft smile on the fern-themed album cover to the wrap-up tone of satisfaction and grin one could swear is audible at the end of the last track, the first *Chico Buarque* is, despite some less than jovial passages, a felicitous work, a glad thirty-three and a third rotations disc, with some clear chords of optimism sans dissonance. The collection of songs from different years in the 1970s encompasses sonic reflections of change over time, particularly in the dark days of the early to mid-decade and at the beginning of the positive turning point in Brazilian history that was the political opening called *abertura*, which had its impacts on popular music and expressive culture at large. While Chico has continued his career in music for more than forty years after the 1978 LP, it can be regarded as the culmination of an absolutely exceptional first decade-plus in the field. By the late seventies, he was already an institution unto himself in Brazil. He was, for many, the top figure in the trend labeled MPB, but comparisons to other prime singer-songwriters were (and still are) common. I was once asked to ponder the comparative merits of the singer-songwriters of the pantheon in Brazil. I skirted the delicate critical predicament by pleading that "all is relative" but offered to speculate in multiple terms that the most beloved figure was Milton Nascimento, the hippest Caetano Veloso, the most venerated Gilberto Gil, and the most admired, Chico Buarque.[1] But what of his status abroad, in 1978 and following years?

The veteran music-researcher and radio programmer in Madrid, Carlos Galilea judged Chico Buarque to be "a singer-songwriter of the importance of a Dylan in English, a Brel in French, or a Serrat in Spanish. Artists with a special gift to capture and reflect in their songs people's problems and feelings."[2] That assessment is certainly pertinent with respect to "Trocando em miudos" and "Pivete" and the whole of the 1978 album on which they appeared together. On that LP, there is another outreach to Portugal, where, no surprise here, the carioca Chico has always been a special draw, having done many shows and television specials. In France, we saw that an aware street band played his most enduring "protest song" in 2016, but over the years he has played and recorded live in Paris and Montreux (well, Switzerland), and he is certainly a known quantity. Since he spent part of his childhood in Italy, as well as eighteen months of "voluntary exile" (1969–70) in which he recorded with Enio Morricone and others, he has a permanent second home there. In the early 1980s, musicologist Paolo Scarnecchia could not resist making a choice for "best in MPB," and owing to the "elusive, ineffable verses and melodies," he selected Chico Buarque.[3]

---

[1] Charles A. Perrone, Elizabeth Ginway and Ataide Tartari, "Chico Buarque sob a ótica internacional." In Fernandes, *Textos,* p. 212.

[2] Carlos Galilea Nin, *Canta Brasil* (Madrid: Ediciones Cúbicas, 1990), p. 55.

[3] Scarnecchia, p. 191. In the twenty-first century, the leading Chico specialist in Italy is Luca Bacchini.

Outro: Rio, Brazil, the World

As his full surname is Buarque de Hollanda, it is logical for there to be an interest in him in Holland. He has been translated, both song lyrics and fiction, into Dutch, and is as well known as other MPB acts. In the late 1980s, Chico played some huge shows in the Netherlands. In Germany, too, attention has been paid. Critical notice was solidified with the work of Claus Scheiner.[4] Could it matter that the dramatic "O malandro" was Chico's version of the German original of "Mack the Knife," "Die Moritat von Mackie Messer" (Kurt Weill-Bertolt Brecht)? Since 2014, the Brazilian's work has renewed interest there as his latest novel is no less than *My German Brother*.

In the other extra-large international arena that is Japan, there is plenty to point to in the Chico Buarque department. With his varied repertory, he has been able to ride a wave of general interest there. Japan is the largest consumer market outside the home country for samba, MPB, and especially bossa nova. Unlike other stars of Brazilian popular music, Chico has never done a performance tour in Japan, yet he is well known in aficionado domains and discussed by the specialized press in such venues as *Latina*, the long-standing Latin American music magazine. Local samba artists specifically cite admiration for Chico as songwriter.[5]

In the United Kingdom, there are constituencies favorable to Chico's musical artistry: some attuned to so-called "world

---

[4] Schreiner, *Música Brasileira* [1977, 1985 German].

[5] https://fjsp.org.br/agenda/bossa-nova-in-japan;https://www.diretodojapao.info/post/2017/12/26/japonesesmusica2017. Accessed January 4, 2021. I am grateful to Professor Shuhei Hosokawa for sharing his knowledge of Brazilian music in Japan. On locals, Shanna Lorenz, "Japanese in the Samba: Japanese-Brazilian Musical Citizenship, Racial Consciousness, and Transnational Migration." PhD dissertation, University of Pittsburgh, 2007, p. 50.

music," others with socialist sympathies, and ex-pat/migrant communities. Since 1969, when England agreed to receive Gil and Caetano as political exiles, there has naturally been greater response to them, especially since they mingled in circles of musicians and recorded new material. Rosane Carneiro Ramos, a sensitive poet, lecturer and Ph D in literature at Kings College London, has reminisced about her experience with the first *Chico Buarque*. As a pre-teen living in Vila Isabel—the turf of Noel Rosa, the Chico Buarque of the late 1920s–mid 1930s— she perceived that the adults really loved the latter; they belted out his songs, especially "Apesar de você." She liked the songs on this LP a lot; she adored "Homenagem ao malandro" and "Tanto mar." There was something in "Cálice" that was intriguing; she sensed the gravity of the music. Years later in college she understood better the importance of the work. "Um álbum tão importante que muitas canções são popularíssimas até hoje. Praticamente são eternas." "An album so important that many songs are very popular to this day. They are practically eternal."[6] Nicely put.

In the Americas, it is safe to say that Chico is the main man of MPB (not counting a pop crooner like Roberto Carlos) in Spanish America. In Chapter 8, we saw the Cuban connection via "Pequeña serenata diurna." There were plenty of Mexican aficionados in the 1970s. The Southern Cone nations where "new song" was important in the seventies, all identified with him. The great voice of Argentina Mercedes Sosa sang with Chico, several of his songs were done in Chile, and the outstanding songsmith Daniel Viglietti of Uruguay wrote

---

[6] Rosane Carneiro Ramos, personal correspondence, 2-17-21.

Spanish versions for the 1982 album *Chico Buarque em español*, which included "A pesar de Usted."

The United States is a different story. After the success of so many bossa nova artists, several of the MPB generation tried their luck in the North American market. In the 1960s, Jorge Ben ("Mas, que nada!"), Edu Lobo (presented by Sérgio Mendes), and Milton Nascimento (a pair of LPs) were able to make some inroads. But no Chico Buarque, despite his association with Tom Jobim. In the 1970s, Gilberto Gil, with the super LP *Nightingale*, and others, but no Chico Buarque. In the 1980s and 1990s, Ivan Lins, Caetano Veloso, the Tropicalist Tom Zé, and others.[7] But no Chico Buarque, who, save an in-transit airport stopover, has never spent time in the United States, much less for a performance or recording engagement. But there are a few moments of Chico reception and recognition in the United States to be taken into account. When David Byrne launched his influential series Brazil Classics in 1989 (initially on tape, LP and CD) with the MPB anthology *Beleza Tropical,* he included "Cálice" and "Caçada" (Hunt), part of Chico's soundtrack for the film *Quando o carnaval chegar* (When carnival comes, 1972). Caetano, by comparison, had four selections. On the subsequent anthology, *O samba* (later in 1989), however, there was no "Feijoada completa" or any other Chico samba.

As for Caetano, he has been back to New York many times since the 1980s; on one occasion he was asked to write for the *New York Times* on Carmen Miranda for an upcoming museum show, after, he reveals in his memoir, their first choice

[7] See Mc Gowan and Pessanha, *Brazilian Sound*, pp. 190–3, on Brazilian artists in the United States.

had "proved unavailable," the recommended Chico Buarque.[8] The book was translated for an Anglophone audience, but, tellingly, the original chapter "Chico" was deleted, with some passages being distributed to other chapters. For his part, lyricist and version-maker Carlos Rennó has figured that it is harder to render Chico's lyrics into English (tell me about it) than it is to write versions of Cole Porter in Portuguese. For such technical reasons, and others, he relates that Caetano told some North American interlocutors that "Chico Buarque is greater than Cole Porter."[9]

The *New York Times* journalist stationed in Brazil at the end of the twentieth century, after reading that Chico was voted the "musician of the century," marveled at his skill and exultant protest, quoting Chico: "Even the handful of my songs most often cited as examples of political resistance are sambas with a happy sound," he said. "People may be protesting, but they are dancing while they do it." This allusion surely includes sambas on the 1978 LP. But more to the point, the US writer calls him "Brazilian music's best kept secret" as he has "little projection abroad," by which he must mean principally in North America,

---

[8] Caetano Veloso, *Tropical Truth: A Story of Music and Revolution in Brazil* (New York: Knopf, 2002), p. 331; abridged trans. of *Verdade Tropical* (São Paulo: Companhia das Letras, 1997). The original word concerning Chico's non-availability is actually *inviabilidade* (inviability, i.e. not a viable option), a bit more insinuating. The book project was in fact inspired by the writing for the *New York Times*, who edited his manuscript down. A translation of the whole of what he originally wrote is a segment in Charles A. Perrone and Christopher Dunn, eds. *Brazilian Popular Music and Globalization* (Gainesville: University of Florida Press, 2001), pp. 39–45.

[9] Carlos Rennó, *O voo das palavras cantadas* (São Paulo: Dash Editora, 2014), p. 128. He earlier published a book of songs, versions: *Cole Porter—Canções, Versões* (São Paulo: Paulicéia, 1991), later expanded (2002) to include George Gershwin.

and quotes a reliable source from whom we heard in the first segment of the body the present study, the intro:

> "Chico is today the most complete artist in Brazilian popular music, a genius of a lyricist, a marvelous melodist and a singer with a very personal voice and timbre," said Almir Chediak, editor of the *Chico Buarque Song Book*, which is to be published here this year. "He is modern in the very best sense of the word, but his music is eternal. So long as there is a Brazil, people are going to be singing the songs of Chico Buarque."[10]

That word again. Eternal. Indeed, the finest hits of the master truly stand the test of time, they can be invoked over and over. As the last of the eleven songs invented for the first *Chico Buarque* intoned repeatedly "vou até o fim," I'm going 'til the end, whether of the immediate performance, an imaginary personal journey, or the open angles of a singer-songwriter's extended timeline. It may have been the final tune on board, but it can be heard to set the tone for persevering appeal.

Finally, one problem with writing about a specific aspect of the work of Chico Buarque is that one wants to cover the whole career and all the marvels, but that, alas, is not the burden here. We have limited ourselves to one 33 1/3 LP with its connections and repercussions. But there will always be another day to do more. Tomorrow will always be another day to recall and to listen to the first *Chico Buarque*.

---

[10] Larry Rohter, "From Rebellion to Romance: A Troubadour Endures." *New York Times,* June 17, 1999.

Bibliography

Ayer, Mauricio. https://outraspalavras.net/mauricioayer/chico-
    buarque-e-a-cachaca-1-o-trabalhador-em-festa/ Molhando
    a palavra: literatura e cachaça com Mauricio Ayer Posted
    7/30/2020.

Bahiana, Ana Maria and Chico Buarque. "Cara nova disco novo."
    O globo. November 12, 1978. Chico Buarque archive at www.
    jobim.org/chico.

Barros e Silva, Fernando de. *Chico Buarque.* São Paulo: Publifolha,
    2004.

Candido, Antonio. *On Literature and Society.* Trans. and preface
    Howard S. Becker. Princeton, NJ: Princeton University Press,
    1995.

Carvalho, Martha Ulhôa de. "Canção da América—Style and
    Emotion in Brazilian Popular Song." *Popular Music.* vol. 9, no. 3
    (1990): 321–49.

Casaus, Victor and Luis Rogelio Nogueras, eds. *Silvio: que levante
    la mano la guitarra.* La Habana: Editorial Letras Cubanas, 2002
    [Instituto Cubano del Libro, 1984].

Chediak, Almir. *Songbook Bossa Nova.* Rio de Janeiro: Lumiar,
    1994.

Chediak, Almir. *Songbook Chico Buarque,* vols. 1, 2, 3. Rio de
    Janeiro: Lumiar, 1999.

Connor, Anne. "Poema de Sete+ Traduções: A Study of Carlos
    Drummond de Andrade's 'Poema de Sete Faces'". *Delos: A
    Journal of Translation and World Literature.* vol. 32 (2017):
    40–59.

Correa, Priscila Gomes. "Performance e resistência no Festival
    Phono 73." *Annals of XXIX Simpósio de História Nacional: contra*

os preconceitos: história de democracia. https://www.snh2017.
    anpuh.org/site/anais.

Crook, Larry. *Brazilian Music: Northeastern Traditions and the
    Heartbeat of a Modern Nation*. Santa Barbara: ABC Clio, 2005.

DaMatta, Roberto. *Carnivals, Rogues, and Heroes: An Interpretation
    of the Brazilian Dilemma*. Trans. John Drury. Notre Dame, IN:
    University of Notre Dame Press, 1992.

Dassin, Joan. "Press Censorship How and Why." *Index of Censorship*.
    vol. 4 (1979): 13–19.

Dinis, Julio. "Chico Buarque—meu falso mentiroso." In Sylvia
    Cyntrão, ed. *Chico Buarque, sinal aberto*. Rio de Janeiro: 7
    Letras, 2015. 183–200.

Diniz, Sheyla Castro. "Denúncia política e contracultura: o show
    'proibido' de Gilberto Gil na Poli / USP (1973)." *Teoria e cultura*.
    vol. 13, no. 2 (2018): 159–74.

Dunn, Christopher J. *Brutality Garden: Tropicália and the
    Emergence of a Brazilian Counterculture*. Chapel Hill, NC:
    University of North Carolina Press, 2001.

Fernandes, Rinaldo, ed. *Chico Buarque do Brasil: textos sobre as
    canções, o teatro, e a ficção de um artista brasileiro*. Rio de
    Janeiro: Editora Garamond, 2004.

Fernandes, Rinaldo, ed. *Chico Buarque: o poeta das mulheres, dos
    desvalidos e dos perseguidos: ensaios sobre a mulher, o pobre e a
    repressão militar nas canções de Chico*. São Paulo: LeYa, 2013.

Fonseca, Aleilton. "Cálice que não se cala", in Fernandes, *Poeta*,
    31–42.

Fontes, Maria Helena Sansão. *Sem fantasia: masculino-feminino
    em Chico Buarque*. Rio de Janeiro: Graphia, 2003.

Galilea Nin, Carlos. *Canta Brasil*. Madrid: Ediciones Cúbicas, 1990.

Gambarra, Rafaela. *Turismo musical no Rio de Janeiro*. Lisbon:
    Chiado, 2018.

Garcia, Luiz Henrique Assis. "Na esquina do mundo: trocas culturais na música popular brasileira através da obra do Clube da Esquina." PhD thesis. Federal University of Minas Gerais, 2006.

Garcia, Tânia da Costa. *The Latin American Songbook in the Twentieth Century: From Folklore to Militancy.* New York: Lexington, 2019.

Garcia, Walter. "Notas sobre 'Cálice' (2010, 1973, 1978, 2011)." *Música popular em revista.* vol. 2, no. 2 (2014): 110–50.

Gil, Gilberto Gil. *Todas as letras.* Carlos Rennó, ed. São Paulo: Companhia das Letras, 1996.

Grasse, Jonathon. *The Corner Club.* New York: Bloomsbury, 2020.

Green, James N. *We Cannot Remain Silent: Opposition to the Brazilian Military Dictatorship in the United States.* Durham, NC: Duke University Press, 2010.

Hertzmann, Marc. *Gilberto Gil's* Refazenda. New York: Bloomsbury, 2020.

Hime, Francis. Interview. *Correio braziliense* on line. November 26, 2017.

Hime, Joana Levenroth. "Uma biografia a dois (Francis e Francisco) 12 anos de parceria." MA thesis, PUC-Rio de Janeiro, 2016.

Homem, Wagner. *Histórias de canções Chico Buarque.* São Paulo: LeYa, 2009.

Johnson, Randal and Robert Stam, eds. *Brazilian Cinema.* Expanded edition. New York: Columbia University Press, 1995 (1982).

Kehl, Maria Rita. "Chico Buarque." In Arthur Nestrovski, ed. *Música popular brasileira hoje.* São Paulo: Publifolha, 2002. 60–2.

Lichote, Leonardo. "Chico e Gil voltam a cantar 'Cálice' juntos após 45 anos." *O globo.* July 29, 2018.

Livingston-Isenhour, Tamara Elena and Thomas George Caracas Garcia. *Choro: A Social History of a Brazilian Popular Music*. Bloomington: Indiana University Press, 2005.

Luz, Leandro Moreira da, Bruno Flávio Lontra Fagundes, and Mônica Luiza Sócio Fernandes. "The Samba Controversy between Noel Rosa and Wilson Batista: Intertextuality and the Meanders of Composition." *Bakhtiniana: Revista de Estudos do Discurso*. vol. 10, no. 2 (2015): 36–53. https://doi.org/10.1590/2176-457320986.

McCann, Bryan. "Noel Rosa's Nationalist Logic." *Luso-Brazilian Review*. vol. 38, no. 1 (2001): 1–16.

McCann, Bryan. *Hello, Hello, Brazil: Popular Music in the Making of Modern Brazil*. Durham: Duke University Press, 2004.

McGowan, Chris. *The Brazilian Music Book: Brazil's Singers, Songwriters and Musicians Tell the Story of Bossa Nova, MPB, and Brazilian Jazz and Pop*. Santa Monica: Culture Planet, 2012.

McGowan, Chris and Ricardo Pessanha. *The Brazilian Sound: Samba, Bossa Nova and the Popular Music of Brazil*. Revised and expanded edition. Philadelphia: Temple University Press, 2009.

Mello, Zuza Homem de. *A era dos festivais: uma parábola*. São Paulo: editora 34 Letras, 2003.

Meneses, Adélia Bezerra de. "Dois guris—ou a maternidade ferida'". in Fernandes, *Poeta*,19–30.

Meneses, Adélia Bezerra de. *Desenho mágico: poesia e política em Chico Buarque*. São Paulo: Hucitec, 1982.

Meneses, Adélia Bezerra de. "Chico Buarque: The Creator and the Revelator." Chediak. vol. 3 (1999): 18–29.

Meneses, Adélia Bezerra de. *Figuras do feminino na canção de Chico Buarque*. São Paulo: Ateliê, 2000.

Moby, Alberto. *Sinal fechado: a música popular brasileira sob censura*. Rio de Janeiro: Obra Aberta, 1994.

Monteiro, Luciana C. "Cross-dressed Poetics: Lessons and Limits of Gender Transgression in Brazilian Popular Music." MA Thesis, University of Florida, 2007.

Monteiro, Pedro Meira. *The Other Roots: Wandering Origins in Roots of Brazil and the Impasses of Modernity in Ibero-America.* Trans. Flora Thomson-Deveaux. Notre Dame, IN: University of Notre Dame Press, 2017.

Moutinho, Marcelo. *Cançoes do Rio: a cidade em letra e música.* Rio de Janeiro: Casa da Palavra, 2010.

Murphy, John P. *Music in Brazil: Experiencing Music, Expressing Culture.* New York: Oxford University Press, 2006.

Napolitano, Marcos. "Hoje preciso refletir um pouco: ser social e e tempo histórico na obra de Chico Buarque de Hollanda 1971/1978." *História São Paulo.* vol. 22, no. 1 (2003): 115–34.

Napolitano, Marcos. "Brazilian Popular Music: The Soundtrack of the Political Opening (1975/1982)." *Estudos Avançados.* vol. 24, no. 69 (2010): 389–402. Original English.

Perrone, Charles A. Elizabeth Ginway and Ataide Tartari. "Chico Buarque sob a ótica internacional." In Fernandes, *textos*, 211–28.

Perrone, Charles A. "Dissonance and Dissent: The Musical Dramatics of Chico Buarque." *Latin American Theater Review.* vol. 22, no. 2 (1989): 81–94.

Perrone, Charles A. "A força dos elos da 'Corrente'." In Fernandes, *Poeta*, 91–8.

Perrone, Charles A. *Masters of Contemporary Brazilian Song: MPB 1965–1985.* Austin: University of Texas Press, 1989.

Perrone, Charles A. *Seven Faces: Brazilian Poetry since Modernism.* Durham: Duke University Press, 1996.

Perrone, Charles A. "Capital Lyric: Poetry and Song in Contemporary Rio de Janeiro and Salvador, Bahia." *Review— Literature and Arts of the Americas.* vol. 83 (2011): 212–22.

Perrone, Charles A. and Christopher Dunn. *Brazilian Popular Music and Globalization*, eds. Gainesville, FL: University of Florida Press, 2001.

Pinto, Fabiane Batista. "O Brasil de Chico Buarque: nação memória e povo." Master's thesis, Sociology, 2007. Universidade Fdederal do Ceará. Fortaleza CE.

Rennó, Carlos. *O vôo das palavras cantadas*. São Paulo: Dash Editora, 2014.

Ribeiro, Renato Janine. "A utopia lírica de Chico Buarque de Hollanda." In Berenice Cavalcante et al, eds. *Decantando a República: inventário histórico e político da canção popular moderna brasileira*. vol. 1. Rio de Janeiro: Nova Fronteira, 2004. 149–68.

Rohter, Larry. "From Rebellion to Romance: A Troubadour Endures." *New York Times,* June 17, 1999.

Rodríguez Silvio. "Chico Buarque es un gran artista." In Fernandes, *Textos*, 59.

Sanches, Pedro Alexandre. *Tropicalismo: decadência bonita do samba*. São Paulo: Boitempo, 2000.

Sandroni, Carlos, "Farewell to MPB." In Idelber Avelar and Christopher Dunn, eds. *Brazilian Popular Music and Citizenship*. Durham, NC: Duke University Press, 2011. 64–73.

Scarnecchia, Paolo. *Musica Popolare Brasiliana*. Milano: Gammalibri, 1983.

Schreiner, Claus. *Música Brasileira: A History of the Popular Music and the People of Brazil*. London: Marion Boyars, 1993 [1977, 1985 German].

Severiano, Jairo and Zuza Homem de Mello. *A canção no tempo: 85 anos de músicas brasileiras. Vol. 2 1958–1985*. São Paulo: editora 34, 1998.

Shaw, Lisa. "Samba and Brasilidade: Notions of National Identity in the Lyrics of Noel Rosa." *Lusotopie* 2002/2: 81–96.

Spiller, David. *Great Singers of the 20th Century*. Independent (Amazon Kindle). 2020.

Stroud, Sean. *The Defence of Tradition in Brazilian Popular Music: Politics, Culture and the Creation of* Música Popular Brasileira. Burlington, VT: Ashgate 2008.

Tatit, Luiz. *O cancionista: composição de canções no Brasil*. São Paulo: EDUSP, 1996.

Luiz Tatit, "Tensões da dor." In Rinaldo Fernandes, ed. *Chico Buarque do Brasil: textos sobre as canções, o teatro, e a ficção de um artista brasileiro* (Rio de Janeiro: Editora Garamond, 2004), 305–12.

Treece, David. *Brazilian Jive From Samba to Bossa and Rap*. London: Reaktion Books, 2013.

Treece. David. "Bringing Brazil's Resistance Songs to London: Words and Music in Translation." *Veredas: Revista da Associação Internacional de Lusitanistas* (2018). 68–84.

Vasconcelos, Francisco de Assis Guedes de, Mariana Perrelli Vasconcelos, and Iris Helena Guedes de Vasconcelos. "Hunger, Food and Drink in Brazilian Popular Music: A Brief Overview." *História, Ciências, Saúde-Manguinhos*. vol. 22, no. 3 (2015). https://doi.org/10.1590/S0104-59702015000300004.

Vasconcellos, Gilberto. *Música popular: de olho na fresta*. Rio de Janeiro: Graal, 1977.

Veloso, Caetano. *Tropical Truth: A Story of Music and Revolution in Brazil*. New York: Knopf, 2002 Trans. of *Verdade tropical*. São Paulo: Companhia das Letras, 1997.

Vianna, Luiz Fernando. "Phono 73 registra história da MPB." *Folha de São Paulo*. November 15, 2005.

Werneck, Humberto. "Gol de letras." In Chico Buarque, *Letra e música*. São Paulo: Companhia das Letras, 1989. 9–264.

Wisnik, José Miguel. *Sem receita, ensaios e canções*. São Paulo: Publifolha, 2004.

Zappa, Regina. *Chico Buarque para todos*. Rio de Janeiro: Relume Dumará Prefeitura do Rio de Janeiro, 2000.

Index